D1082721

Hannah Arendt

Martin Heidegger

Hannah Arendt

Martin Heidegger

Elżbieta Ettinger

Yale University Press

New Haven and London

Published with assistance from the foundation established in memory of Philip Hamilton McMillan of the Class of 1894, Yale College.

Library of Congress Cataloging-in-Publication Data
Ettinger, Elżbieta.
Hannah Arendt / Martin Heidegger / Elżbieta Ettinger.
    p.   cm.
Includes bibliographical references (p.   ) and index.
ISBN 0-300-06407-1 (cloth : alk. paper)
1. Heidegger, Martin, 1889-1976—Friends and associates.   2. Arendt, Hannah—Friends and associates.   I. Title.
B3279.H49E88   1995
193—dc20
[B]   95-2469
                        CIP

A catalogue record for this book is available from the British Library.

The paper in this book meets the guidelines for permanence and durability of the Committee on Production Guidelines for Book Longevity of the Council on Library Resources.

10   9   8   7   6   5   4   3

To my daughter, Maia Ettinger, and to her father, Manfred Lachs

C o n t e n t s

A c k n o w l e d g m e n t s

I am grateful to the Hannah Arendt Literary Trust, New York City; the Library of Congress, Washington, D.C.; and Deutsches Literaturarchiv, Marbach am Neckar, Germany, for permission to use their archives.

I wish to express my sincerest thanks to Hugo Ott and Inge Wissner.

Dagmar Barnouw, Isaiah Berlin, Udo Brandhorst, Maia Ettinger, Walter Grossmann, Melvyn Hill, Gerald Holton, Nina Holton, Irving Howe, Roman Kaufmann, Alfred Kazin, Mary McCarthy, Kenneth R. Manning, Misha Pankratov, Anette Peterson-Brandhorst, Agneta Pleijel, Marcel Reich-Ranicki, Claire Rosenfield, Brigitte Seebacher-Brandt, Janna Malamud Smith, Fritz Stern, Aileen Ward, and Elisabeth Young-Bruehl were helpful in ways perceptible and imperceptible.

Georges Borchardt, my agent, served with wise advice and with patience.

Jonathan Brent, my editor, gave me inestimable help, not only in editing.

Introduction

Hannah Arendt and Martin Heidegger met in 1924 when Arendt, an eighteen-year-old German Jewess, enrolled at the University of Marburg and attended his classes in philosophy. Their relationship—a word that inadequately conveys the depth of their bond—was to last half a century. What started as a passionate love affair underwent many transformations over the years. To say that it turned into a friendship is to say both too much and too little, though both Arendt and Heidegger might have called it just that. Arendt captured the impossibility of categorizing her emotions when she confessed to Heidegger, in an unsent note, that he was the man "to whom I remained faithful and unfaithful, and both in love."[1] She was at the time fifty-four years old; he was past seventy.

The relationship can be roughly divided into three phases: 1925 until 1930 or so, when the two were lovers; the early 1930s (Heidegger joined the Nazi Party in 1933) until 1950, when their lives were utterly changed by the rise of National Socialism and the Second World War; and 1950 to 1975, when, at Arendt's initiative, they resumed their old relationship—or, rather, built a new one—that lasted until Hannah Arendt died.

Throughout their relationship each depended on the other in ways as different as their lives, needs, and personalities. The young Arendt needed love, protection, guidance. When she was seven her father died of syphilis, and shortly before that she had lost her paternal grandfather, to whom she was deeply attached. Her adored mother traveled frequently to take the waters or visit relatives, and each absence left the child upset, fearing that her mother would not return. Martha Arendt remarried when Hannah was thirteen. The marriage wreaked havoc in Hannah's life: she had to share her mother not only with a man who remained a stranger to her but also with two older stepsisters she detested but to whom her mother felt close. From childhood, the world was a bewildering place to Hannah, not least because of her Jewish origin, for years an enigma and a source of confusion. She felt lost, helpless, unprotected, yet she always put up a brave front. "This idiotic compulsion," she wrote to her husband, Heinrich Bluecher, in 1945, "inbred since youth, always to put up an act in front of the world . . . pretending everything is just fine, that's what consumes much of my energy."[2]

The adult Arendt, the preeminent scholar, would indeed appear to the world self-confident, even imperious. But never would she appear so to Heidegger.

The first-year student found in Heidegger a lover, friend, teacher, and protector. He promised to love her forever, to help and guide her. Carried away by his seductive declarations, she let down her defenses as never before: in an unpublished confessional piece, written in 1925, that she called "The Shadows" (*Die Schatten*), she described for him the terrors of her childhood and girlhood, her insecurity and vulnerability.

When they met, the thirty-five-year-old Heidegger, married and the father of two young sons, was finishing the manuscript of *Being and Time* (Sein und Zeit, 1927), a book that would put him in the ranks of the most prominent philosophers of the twentieth century. From their correspondence it is clear that he fell in love with his young student from their earliest meetings in his classroom. And though his passion subsided as time went on, his need to be her idol did not. Until he met Hannah, Heidegger—strict, rigid, hard-working, the son of devout Catholic peasants—seems to have known little of genuine passion, of a physical and spiritual bond. It is clear from Heidegger's letters to Arendt that she showed him how to love ardently and not feel it a sin. He needed her in order to breathe fully and deeply, to enjoy being alive; he needed to have her as a "stimulating force" in his life, as he put it.

Despite the obstacles—Heidegger's family and his university position were the most serious ones—their mutual needs were fulfilled throughout the first phase of their relationship. Their need for each other never disappeared completely, though the following seventeen years changed the world as profoundly as they changed each of them.

In August 1933, four months after Heidegger was appointed rector of the Albert-Ludwigs-University in Freiburg, joined the Nazi Party, and delivered his notorious Rectorial Address, identifying himself with and supporting the ideology of the Party, Hannah Arendt left Germany. Though exile had already been on Arendt's mind, and though she had been briefly detained by the police in Berlin, Heidegger's openly declared allegiance to Adolf Hitler shattered whatever illusions she still might have had about him and may well have precipitated her decision. Henceforth she would blame the German intellectuals, including Heidegger, for supporting Hitler, for betraying Western culture, for displaying blindness and cowardice.

For Arendt, brought up in a completely assimilated social democratic family in Koenigsberg, the "Jewish question" was limited to the name-calling of street urchins and schoolchildren or to the occasional antisemitic remark of a teacher.* According to her mother's instructions, she had to

*In a 1964 interview Arendt said: "As a child I did not know that I was Jewish. . . . The word 'Jew' was never mentioned at home when I was a child. As a child, now a slightly older one, I knew that I looked Jewish. That is, I looked different from all the others." *Gespraeche mit Hannah Arendt,* Adelbert Reif, ed. (Munich: Piper, 1976), 15–16.

defend herself only from the children; her mother dealt with the teachers. In a 1952 letter to her mentor Karl Jaspers, Arendt claimed that by virtue of her background she was "simply naïve" and that she found the Jewish question "boring" until her early twenties, when it became a political issue.[3] Her scholarly interests may perhaps serve as an indication of the change she underwent: in 1928, when she completed her doctoral dissertation on St. Augustine, she began research for a biography of Rahel Varnhagen, a book first published in London in 1958 as *Rahel Varnhagen: The Life of a Jewess.* Rahel Varnhagen, née Lewin (1771–1833), was famous for her intellectual salon, but the indignities and humiliations she suffered as a German Jew interested Arendt most. Her research for this book led to her preoccupation with the causes of antisemitism and with the history of the German Jews and her place in it.

Thus, while Heidegger supported the cause of National Socialism as rector of Freiburg University (April 1933 to April 1934), Arendt, in exile, was finishing the biography and working for Youth Alijah, an organization that trained Jewish youth for agricultural labor in Palestine. She also was gathering material for what was to become *The Origins of Totalitarianism,* a substantial part of which explored the history of antisemitism.

Heidegger had found a like-minded companion in his wife, Elfride, a zealous Nazi since the 1920s. In 1936 Arendt met a former German communist in exile, Heinrich Bluecher, who became her second husband, her soul mate and secure haven. (Her 1929 marriage to Guenther Stern formally ended in 1937.)

When Arendt met Heidegger again in 1950 (at this time the extent of his collaboration with the Nazi regime had not been made public), he needed Arendt for purposes entirely different from before. The ban on his teaching, the five-year battle to clear his name, and the collapse of his hopes to "rejuvenate" Germany by rescuing it from the onslaught of technology, decadence, and communism had left Heidegger bitter and disappointed but not penitent. He welcomed Arendt back into his life with genuine joy. But her horror over his alleged antisemitism and his pro-Nazi activities did not bode well for the reunion. Still, she came and listened to him, and he easily convinced her that the accusations were nothing but slander. Arendt was overcome with happiness. Her decision to return to her friend and mentor, to the man she still loved, though differently from before, was right. To miss the chance to revive the continuity of their lives would have been an unexcusable mistake, she subsequently wrote to him.

Heidegger needed her forgiveness, for it absolved him of the charge of antisemitism and restored his confidence in the soundness of his moral principles. Hannah Arendt would be his goodwill ambassador to the world at large, in particular to Karl Jaspers, Heidegger's former close friend and now a friend of Arendt's. She would defend him against what she now believed to be unfounded charges. The prestige she enjoyed in the American intellectual community, of which Heidegger certainly was aware, was a precious asset. For the next twenty-five years their lives remained intertwined. Arendt's husband, an admirer of Heidegger's philosophy if not of him as a person, encouraged her efforts, agreeing with Arendt that all that really mattered was to let Heidegger work in peace. She visited him as often as he would allow, secure in her belief that she alone knew and understood him and therefore that she alone could alleviate his depressions and help him regain the peace of mind necessary for his work. Heidegger kept her abreast of his writings and lectures, and she in turn asked his advice on philosophical matters, not infrequently emphasizing the debt she owed him. A refrain in her letters to him was that her thinking would not have evolved as it had "without what I learned from you in my youth."[4] He inspired her thinking and kept the classical philosophers, her most important teachers, alive and close to her; Arendt and Heidegger derived intense joy from the same works of literature, the same poetry, the same music. And as in the beginning, Heidegger wrote poems for her. Yet beneath this smooth surface ran an undercurrent of highly charged tensions, conflicting emotions, unresolved claims, and rancor on both sides. Hence the long—sometimes years long—lapses in their correspondence and meetings.

In 1974, a year before she died, Arendt wrote to him: "No one can deliver a lecture the way you do, nor did anyone before you."[5] Though Heidegger did not lack accolades, Arendt's dependence on him fulfilled a need that no one else could meet. In the 1940s some of his other disciples, Herbert Marcuse among them, turned away from him not because of his support of National Socialism but because of his adamant refusal to denounce the Party and renounce his membership in it. Arendt, "the passion of his life," posed no such demands.[6] Instead, she devoted herself to popularizing his philosophy in the United States and to vindicating his name in the eyes of his critics. She remained faithful to her first love and kept bringing back to the aging and lonely man an illusion of youth and a sense of being a supreme being in a world drowning in mediocrity.

It is hardly possible to measure the influence Arendt and Heidegger had on each other. There is no doubt, however, that assessing their mutual dependency and the importance each had for the other is a key to understanding their lives.

The picture of Martin Heidegger that emerges from his relationship with Hannah Arendt will no doubt surprise readers familiar with the philosopher's work, especially those who see in Heidegger only an austere and abstract thinker. At times he expresses his emotions in a typically Germanic, almost clichéd romantic vocabulary. His romantic predisposition seems to have led him both to a passionate attachment to Hannah Arendt and to a fascination with the Nazi vision of the rebirth of Germany. It may well be that scholars should look for the origins of Heidegger's involvement with Nazism not only in his philosophy but also in the specific needs of his emotional life. His relationship with Hannah Arendt provides a glimpse into the world of his feelings, which he carefully kept out of sight.

Hannah Arendt

Martin Heidegger

One

In her tribute "Martin Heidegger at Eighty" (1969), Hannah Arendt addressed in an extensive footnote the philosopher's excursion into the "world of human affairs"—that is, his collaboration with the Nazis. She found it "striking and perhaps exasperating that Plato and Heidegger, when they entered into human affairs, turned to tyrants and Fuehrers," and she pointed out that by neglecting to read *Mein Kampf,* "like so many German intellectuals, Nazis and anti-Nazis," Heidegger escaped "from the reality of the Gestapo cellars and the torture hells of the early concentration camps into ostensibly more significant regions."

Arendt defined Heidegger's collaboration with the Nazis

as "[t]his episode, which today . . . is usually called an 'error.'" She referred to "ten short hectic months," although Heidegger was rector of the University of Freiburg from 21 April 1933 to 23 April 1934. It seems improbable that she did not know by 1969 that he had been a member of the National Socialist German Workers Party (NSDAP) from May 1933 until the Party ceased to exist, in May 1945. But she might not have known that Heidegger had read *Mein Kampf* as early as 1931 at the urging of his wife, who thought that "one must put aside everything else and read *Mein Kampf*."[1]

Arendt went to extraordinary pains to minimize and justify Heidegger's contribution to and support of the Third Reich. "Heidegger himself corrected his own 'error' more quickly and more radically than many of those who later sat in judgement over him," she wrote in the tribute. "He took considerably greater risks than were usual in German literary and university life, during that period."[2] None of these statements is borne out by available evidence, and it appears that Arendt uncritically repeated what Heidegger told her at their first reunion in 1950 and at later meetings.

In her tribute to Heidegger, the last act in a drama that started almost half a century earlier, Arendt displayed the same unquestioning generosity, loyalty, and love she had shown since the beginning.

Hannah Arendt was eighteen years old in the late fall of 1924, when she became a student of philosophy at the University of Marburg. Martin Heidegger, completing his major work *Being and Time,* was the most popular teacher at the university because of his innovative philosophical thought and mesmerizing delivery. Karl Loewith recalls that Heidegger was called the "little magician from Messkirch" (his place of birth) by his students. His looks, his costume, his lecturing style all created an aura of uniqueness. "It is rather difficult to describe Heidegger's face," Loewith continues, "because he could never look straight into one's eyes for long. His natural expression revealed a reflective brow, an inscrutable countenance, and downcast eyes, which now and again would cast a quick glance to assess the situation. Forced, in conversation, to look one straight in the face, he would appear reserved and insecure, for he lacked the gift of candid communication with other people. Hence his natural expression was one of cautious, peasant-sly mistrust." He usually dressed in knickerbockers and a folksy Black Forest peasant coat with wide facings and a semi-military collar, both made of dark brown cloth. "The dark color of the cloth matched his jet-black hair and dark complexion. He was a dark little man who knew how to cast a spell. . . . The technique of his lectures consisted in building up a complex structure of ideas, which he then dismantled to confront the overstrung student with a puzzle and leave him in a void. This art of witchcraft entailed very risky results: it attracted more or less psychopathic minds, and one student took her own life after three years of puzzle-solving."[3] Aware of his allure to both male and female students and of his power over their minds, Heidegger purposely kept his distance, intensifying the mystique, the awe, the reverence.

Born in 1889 to Catholic parents of modest means—
"neither rich nor poor," in the words of his brother Fritz—
Martin was destined early to become a priest; thus the cost
of his education was partially financed by the church.[4] Catholic theology leading toward priesthood was Heidegger's
chosen field of study when he graduated from the gymnasium at the age of twenty. The strict discipline imposed on
theology students at the Albert-Ludwigs-University in
Freiburg was for Heidegger merely an extension of his rou-
tine as a boarder at the gymnasium: from early morning until
night his time was assigned to prayer, study in classes, and
homework. From Hugo Ott's biography we learn that in
1911, the second year of his studies, Heidegger suffered a
bout of ill health caused by asthma and a heart condition,
both of a nervous nature. He was already thinking of giving
up theology and studying mathematics or philosophy. This
extremely difficult decision—it meant a drastic change from
a vocation chosen long ago and an end to financial support—
may have caused the nervous affliction. Heidegger was in
crisis, for Catholicism was not only a subject his studies
but also a spiritual destiny, a faith, a stronghold. But once he
made the decision he never turned back, even though the
break remained a disturbing, unresolved conflict throughout
his life. It was to surface in a peculiar way under the Nazis
and, later, when the Catholic Church tried to reclaim him
after the Second World War. In 1913 Heidegger obtained a
doctoral degree in philosophy; in another two years he completed his habilitation thesis, which qualified him for lectur-

ing. After a short-lived engagement to a woman named Margaret, Heidegger in 1917 married Elfride Petri, a student of political economy at Freiburg University and a descendant of Prussian military caste of Evangelic-Lutheran faith. Heidegger's spiritual dilemma provoked another significant decision in 1918: while expecting the birth of their first child, Elfride Heidegger informed Dr. Egelbert Krebs, the priest of the Freiburg archdiocese and an old friend who had married the couple, that after profound soul-searching and prayer the couple could not, in good conscience, baptize the child in the Catholic Church. This was the first time, though by no means the last, that Frau Heidegger represented her husband in a situation he found uncomfortable or embarrassing.

The year 1922 was marked by two important events in Heidegger's life: he was appointed *Extraordinarius* (associate professor) in philosophy at the university in Marburg, and his wife had a wooden cabin built for him in the country, in Todtnauberg, near Freiburg. There, close to nature and to the country people whose presence he preferred to that of the professors, he could think and write.

As is evident from his letters, his encounter with Hannah Arendt in the fall of 1924 was to shatter for many years the established order of his existence. It was to bring out a side of him that he himself did not know existed and make him break the fundamental rules of the respectable social and academic milieu, rules that he had attentively followed. "An inherited reserve and awkwardness," he wrote earlier that year to Karl Jaspers, made it difficult even for a friend to get close to him, but neither of these traits is detectable in his budding relationship with Arendt. "I live in solitude," he said in the same letter, and though solitude was necessary for a thinker, both philosophers desired a kindred spirit with whom to "do philosophy."[5] His young student could not be a partner in philosophical polemics, but she could listen and provide companionship when solitude weighed him down.

In the small university town of Freiburg, where, as Hannah Tillich, the wife of the theologian, recalled in her autobiography, bobbed hair and fashionable clothes drew disapproving glances in the street, it took uncommon determination and perhaps desperation for a married professor and father to engage in an affair with a student. Even exercising the utmost caution and resorting to all kinds of conspiratorial tactics with Hannah's willing and understanding help, Martin Heidegger put his marriage and career at risk. Apparently confident in his ability to avoid suspicion, and unable to resist Arendt, he took that risk. Nor did he shy away from the hazardous practice of writing her letters, so deep, it appears, was his need to talk to her, to put on paper the new emotions and the thoughts her presence or absence evoked in him. The Heidegger who emerges from these letters is a man of intense passions, and the letters themselves—at times deeply sentimental and romantic, at times acid and hurtful—offer fascinating insights into his soul.

Heidegger initiated the affair, as his first letter to Arendt makes clear, with forethought, using his position and maturity to take advantage, to some extent at least, of her innocence and of the overpowering attraction that his intellect and manhood held for her. From the beginning he kept the upper hand, dependent though he was on her love for him.

Heidegger, who was of peasant stock and raised in the provinces, may well have been taken by Hannah's exotic looks, expansive nature, and elegant comportment. The product of the Jewish cosmopolitan milieu, she stood in stark contrast to the Teutonic Brunhildas he was close to: his mother and his wife. He caught her large, dark eyes in the classroom, observed her for about two months, then invited her to a conference in his office. He would fondly recall in his letters the image of Hannah as she came in wearing a raincoat, a hat pulled low over her face, now and then uttering a barely audible "yes" or "no." The meeting was followed by Heidegger's writing a lengthy letter in an elaborate and eloquent prose.

That Hannah Arendt was drawn to him is not surprising. Given the powerful influence he exerted on his students it was almost inevitable. Neither her past—that of a fatherless, searching youngster—nor her vulnerable, melancholic nature prepared her to withstand Heidegger's determined effort to win her heart. She shared the insecurity of many assimilated Jews who were still uncertain about their place, still harboring doubts about themselves. By choosing her as his beloved, Heidegger fulfilled for Hannah the dream of generations of German Jews, going back to such pioneers of assimilation as Rahel Varnhagen.

Heidegger's first letter to Hannah, dated 10 February 1925, bears the formal salutation "Dear Miss Arendt." Keeping a courteous distance he declared his respect for her, praised the qualities of her mind and soul, and asked only that she let him help her to remain faithful to herself. His sensitivity to her youth and needs will keep her restlessness at bay, he promised, and she, in turn, will no doubt comprehend the frightful loneliness of a man devoted exclusively to scholarly pursuits. It is an emotional letter—lyrical, beautifully phrased, a subtle caress and a firm statement. It contains no wavering, no doubts, not even reflections or questions. The letter was well thought through, each word, each phrase, each thought purposeful, suggestive, seductive. It foreshadowed Heidegger's moves and tactics.

In fact, Arendt did not need coaxing. Overwhelmed, if bewildered, she absorbed every word. Heidegger's desire to be her friend and teacher outside of the classroom was the ultimate praise, a gift she could have hardly expected or rejected. Naturally, it was not a companionship of equals (this Hannah took for granted), nor would it ever be. Decades later, after Arendt achieved fame and recognition, he would still treat her at times as an obedient girl student.

The first letter was followed in only four days by another one, this time to "Dear Hannah." Two weeks later Heidegger wrote Arendt a brief note that indicates a turn in their relationship, the beginning of physical intimacy. Gripped by a hitherto unknown emotion, he was like a man possessed.

Hannah Arendt gave her love freely, happily, defying convention. She held up for Heidegger a mirror in which was
reflected an almost godlike being. For the Catholic boy from
Messkirch she personified everything he might have seen in
some perplexing dreams.

To all appearances Heidegger was not an aggressive man,
at least not in the conventional sense. But his willingness to
put his family and career at risk in his pursuit of Hannah
reveals a forceful, self-centered nature and a capacity for
ruthlessness and cunning. Despite this, or maybe because of
it, he was an insecure man in constant need of worship and
adulation—international recognition was still some years
away—which Hannah provided in abundance.

These complexities slowly emerged in his attitude toward
Arendt, but she did not see them any more than she compre-
hended his need to control her, which she probably interpreted as a desire to protect her. Whether by flattery, dis-
plays of devotion, declarations of everlasting love, lyrical
poems, or commands, Heidegger determined the conditions
of their relationship for its duration. That he was capable of
possessing a proud woman already known for her fierce
independence was deeply gratifying.

Her youth and insecurity notwithstanding, Arendt proved
stronger and more resilient than Heidegger in the face of
social convention. There is no evidence to suggest that she
ever thought or wished that Heidegger would leave his family

for her. And even though, after a year of clandestine meetings, she started to think about moving to another university, her love for him did not abate. If anything, it seems to have intensified, just as Heidegger had predicted. The growing intensity of her love scared her and might have pushed her to leave. Did she rebel inwardly against her back-street existence? This seems unlikely, for the aura of mystery was as alluring to her as it was to him.

It is reported that as a young teenager Hannah was fascinated by family tales about a beautiful vanished aunt who, involved in subversive political activities, led a secretive life, surreptitiously crossing frontiers, carrying messages, and being adored by her co-conspirators, who knew her stunning face only from behind a thick veil.[6] As a middle-aged woman writing about Rosa Luxemburg, Arendt emphasized that the compulsion for anonymity of Luxemburg's lover and his fascination for conspiracy and danger enhanced his erotic charm. Yet for all the appeal of secrecy, the excitement over Heidegger's many cryptic notes—summoning her when he expected to be alone, giving the place and the time, down to the exact minute, of their next rendezvous, and the elaborate signals of lights switched on and off—would eventually disappear. Perhaps she was growing uncomfortable with the "girlish" virtues he extolled in her and with her passive role, which mostly amounted to following his orders and keeping silent. It weighed heavily on her that she could not talk with him openly, though Heidegger assured her in one of his letters that she could better reveal her inner self without words. But she could not overcome the almost obsessive shyness his presence induced in her. As he recalled, she would whisper "if you want me," or "if you like," for intuition and experience told her that modesty and mute idolization pleased and excited him. Perhaps she was subconsciously trying to obliterate the stereotype of a Jewess—loud, self-assured, clever—and, like her heroine, Rahel Varnhagen, was seeing the phantoms of her ancestors standing in her way. Yet above all else it may have been her own inhibition and insecurity, aggravated by Heidegger's behavior, his likes and dislikes, that trapped her.

Throughout their love affair Arendt understood and accepted Heidegger's rules. She did everything in her power to ease the burden of his split life, followed every one of his often shifting and complicated instructions concerning their meetings; she was uncomplaining, undemanding, available when he wanted her, patiently waiting when he did not. She cherished the privilege of being his mistress and confidante. He kept her abreast of his work, of the prospects of his university career, of his relations with his mentor Edmund Husserl and his friend Karl Jaspers. And he never tired of impressing on his young student the innate spirituality of the German intellectual elite. At the age of eighteen or nineteen she lived vicariously among creators of ideas, falsely assuming that the mundane world of politics, of everyday reality, was alien to them. Had she been privy to the correspondence between Heidegger and Jaspers, which was carried on concurrently with hers and Heidegger's, she would have been shocked by the philosophers' pragmatism, their careful calculations of salaries, fringe benefits, widow's pensions, and moving expenses as a basis for accepting or rejecting a teaching position, or by Jaspers's decision to accept interest on a short-term loan extended to Heidegger. These banal concerns pale in the face of their involvement in university politicking before and after the Nazi takeover.

In 1926, about a year after Arendt and Heidegger's affair started, Arendt was deeply torn about leaving Marburg. Although it was common for a student to change universities to study or write a doctoral dissertation under a professor of his or her choice, this was not what motivated Arendt. While she apparently wanted to get on with her life, she also wanted to be near Heidegger and to study with him. Perhaps she nurtured the hope that he would dissuade her from leaving once she told him about her decision. Finally, it was his well-being—"because of my love for you, to make nothing more difficult than it already was"—that took precedence over other considerations. Twenty-five years later she told him bluntly: "I left Marburg exclusively because of you."[7]

Yet by the time Arendt told Heidegger that she was considering a move to another university, he had already decided that she must leave Marburg. It is not clear whether his nerves gave in or his wife became suspicious or Arendt's presence became too disruptive, but it is clear that, unlike Arendt, he did not intend to put an end to the affair but merely to reduce the hazards. In January 1926, Heidegger wrote Arendt a letter that puts into serious question his intentions concerning her well-being, which he had expressed in letters one year earlier. In the letter he emphatically refers to "her decision," as though she had already made it, but it seems that she was still wavering. As her teacher he could have attempted to dissuade her from leaving so that she could continue her studies with him. Yet he never did so. Apart from her personal feelings, studying under Heidegger was an enormously serious matter for her, as is evident in *The Human Condition* (1958), which, as she wrote to him, "owes you in every regard, almost everything."[8]

Heidegger, it seems clear, pressured her to leave. He questioned her ability to do her work at Marburg, where, he claimed, she had failed to establish herself and did not fit in. Young people who cannot muster enough strength to quit a school in which they do not belong were wanting, in his opinion. If they insist on staying they forgo the chance to grow, he argued. Nor, he said, is it especially beneficial to be regarded a "Heidegger student"—a bizarre statement coming from a philosopher who had no equal in Germany.

In view of Arendt's reputation as one of the outstanding minds at Marburg, Heidegger's evaluation of her academic standing strains credulity. The teacher who all year long had nothing but praise for her, had discussed his own work with her, and had repeatedly stressed their spiritual kinship now betrayed her for reasons unconnected to her academic performance. If Arendt was the first of his disciples whom Heidegger failed in his professional capacity, she was not the last. During his tenure as rector he blocked the promotion of Eduard Baumgarten because he "was anything but a National Socialist."[9] Later, he effectively put an end to Max Mueller's scholarly career when he accused Mueller of having a negative attitude toward the Third Reich merely because Mueller was a fervent Catholic. Personal, political, and religious reasons, not scholarship, informed many of his decisions. Professor Heidegger was in a position of power. He enjoyed power, and he used it as he saw fit.

The letter of January 1926 might have sown the first doubts in Arendt's mind, though she abruptly brushed them away. Heidegger had assured her that she and her love for him were intrinsic to his work and life. Now he persuasively argued that she must leave if she had the strength and ability to understand what was best for her intellectual growth. Her decision, he wrote, demanded a sacrifice not only from her but from him as well. He was ready to make it for her sake, and the sacrifice might, he thought, enrich them both— spiritually.

Judging from Arendt's letters to Heinrich Bluecher written ten years later, it is safe to assume that only with the passage of time and the wisdom of hindsight could Arendt fully understand the intention behind Heidegger's convoluted arguments. And when she did, her letters disclose, she felt belittled, manipulated, cheated. Yet this would change little in her behavior toward Heidegger.

Arendt did not resist but rather welcomed her role as
Heidegger's apprentice. Her obedience or even passivity
cannot be judged by today's standards but by the prevailing
norms of behavior, which dictated that students treat a professor like a master. Yet to deal with a lover and a professor in
one person could not but deepen Arendt's confusion.

The professor-student relationship at a German university
presupposed not a mentor-disciple attitude so much as a
master-apprentice attitude. In most European educational
institutions the paradigm of the elevated position of the
teacher and the subordinate position of the pupil was firmly
established, and in the German system, structured patterns of
thought and behavior, with Prussian-style discipline and hier-
archy, predominated. A stern father at home had his counter-
part at school. The professor stood literally and figuratively
on a pedestal; the atmosphere in the classroom was solemn,
the etiquette obligatory, the rules of conduct—concerning
dress, looks, manners—strictly observed. Hannah Arendt
experienced culture shock when she first saw the Berkeley
campus some thirty years later; the lack of discipline among
the unkempt and easygoing students did not amuse her. The
give-and-take informality of an American classroom was
alien to her, though with time she came to appreciate it.

Arendt belonged among the young German-Jewish intellectuals who sought in German philosophy a substitute for

religion, and in the philosophers the embodiment of Germanness and of the *Geist*. Heidegger held yet another attraction for them: by reviving and incorporating Greek philosophers into contemporary German thought, he provided students with a way out of cultural dilemmas. This too must have appealed to Arendt, whose desire for Heidegger's protection for her soul was exacerbated by her need for intellectual belonging and cultural acceptance. In the postwar years, when what was seen as Heidegger's betrayal of Western culture was threatening students' own "time and being," some of his students, like Herbert Marcuse, pleaded with the thinker to recant his Nazi past; others absolved him of any wrongdoing. Hannah Arendt was among the latter. She did so, at least in part, it seems, to protect herself, to salvage the Geist her teacher had helped her attain in her youth. Her bond to Heidegger remained even though her life underwent a drastic change: in 1941 she moved to America (a country Heidegger held in contempt for putting materialistic values before spiritual ones and for its preoccupation with technology) and built a life with a man she loved. But, as her former student observed, "even in the presence of his absence" Heidegger remained for her an authority.[10]

Heidegger transferred the cult of worship from the lecture hall to his personal relationship with Arendt. Apparently it was vital for him to maintain a barrier between himself and Arendt, to preserve the master-apprentice relationship, so apprehensive must he have been of either endangering his authority or of letting Arendt get too close to him.

For the first time in his well-regulated life he found himself in an ambivalent situation, and he was groping for ways to deal with it. Throughout their relationship Arendt's role as his student contended with his physical need for her. She consented to the way Heidegger set up their personal relationship and appears to have readily accepted the role he assigned to her. But that role often must have seemed contradictory.

When they were together, taking a walk or meeting on "their" bench, he talked and she listened. As their correspondence suggests, his monologues were about his philosophical thought, ancient and modern philosophy, literature, poetry, music, and nature, topics that had preoccupied Arendt since her early adolescence. They delighted in Bach and Beethoven, Rilke and Thomas Mann (both were enthusiastic about *The Magic Mountain*). His soliloquies on Socrates, Plato, and Heraclitus remained a treasured memory for Arendt.

"The Shadows," the confessional meditation that Arendt wrote as a "gift" for Heidegger in the summer of 1925, shows that she wanted him to know her most intimate thoughts and about her childhood and adolescence, the sources, she thought, of her fears and vulnerability. With its aura of melancholy, restlessness, and disconnectedness, the confession recalls Goethe's *The Sorrows of Young Werther*. In his letters, Heidegger, too, departed from the neutral ground of philosophy and literature. Suffused with sensuous love, his letters show that for him, as for Arendt, it was easier to write about emotions than to speak about them.

For the spring semester of 1926 Arendt moved to Heidelberg to study for a doctorate in philosophy with Karl Jaspers, to whom Heidegger had recommended her, a common practice among professors. Jaspers would sometimes provide Heidegger with information about Arendt, even news of a private nature: it was a little harmless gossip, as Jaspers saw it, but to Heidegger it was important. It was not until 1949 that Jaspers learned from Arendt of their affair.

Arendt left Marburg, but she did not leave Heidegger. She did not give him her new address in Heidelberg, however. Her reasons are not known but may well have had to do with a suspicion that his love stemmed merely from physical attraction, while she was in love with both the man and his mind. As if commenting on her earlier relationship with Heidegger, she wrote to Bluecher some ten years later: "It still seems unbelievable to me that I can have both, the 'great love,' and retain my own identity. And only now I have the former since I also have the latter. Finally, I know what happiness actually is."[11]

Heidegger wanted to get in touch with Arendt in the least conspicuous way. He did not dare address a letter to the Heidelberg University, and to ask Jaspers how to reach her seemed too risky. In the end, Heidegger's student and Arendt's friend, Hans Jonas, gave Heidegger her address. The correspondence as well as the meetings resumed, apparently with Arendt's cooperation. She might well have been waiting for a sign from him, unwilling to make the first step. Now Heidegger made even more elaborate plans than before: she was to meet him in a small town, say, Weinheim, on his way from Freiburg to Switzerland. He would travel from Marburg to Freiburg on Wednesday, 4 April, and proceed on 6 April from Freiburg to Switzerland. He invited her as his guest, presumably to a hotel. Unsure of whether his letter would reach her in time and whether she would be free but convinced that she would be willing to see him, he asked her to send him a postcard with greetings commemorating the end of the semester to signal that his plan was workable, and he promised to look for her at all the little stations where his train made brief stops.

After a time their correspondence and their meetings became more sporadic. Months would go by with no communication, and Heidegger initiated whatever communication there was. He wrote to Arendt that her letters substituted for her presence; increasingly, he held her "dear hands" in imagination more often than in the flesh. And he kept praying for her happiness.

First from Jaspers and then from Arendt, Heidegger learned at the beginning of 1928 about a man in her life, a fellow student named Benno von Wiese. Jaspers, who liked both students, told Heidegger that they were engaged to be married—a perfect marriage, he thought. It is doubtful that either Arendt or von Wiese thought about a permanent union. In fact, the affair was short-lived (1927 to 1928) and may have represented to Arendt little more than an attempt at displacing Heidegger. Although she worked hard for Jaspers, who was an extremely demanding teacher, and now had a male companion, her decision to inform Heidegger about von Wiese shows that Heidegger was still on her mind. She assured him that she was happy, and that announcement brought an outburst of joy (or relief), blessings, and good wishes from Heidegger, but it did not stop him from pursuing her. Once, probably in 1928, Arendt went for a long-planned tour of Nürenberg and its environs with her close friend Kaete Levin. In the midst of the trip she received, she told her companion, a letter from Heidegger summoning her to a rendezvous. Without a moment's hesitation she interrupted the trip, left Kaete, and rushed to meet Heidegger.[12]

No sooner would Arendt achieve a precarious balance in her new life with von Wiese than Heidegger would send her a letter or note filled with memories of their shared past and assurances of his abiding love and constant longing for her. Heidegger had forbidden her to respond to his letters unless he asked her to do so, which he did from time to time. Arendt wrote these letters "on order," not without effort, it seems. When he kept silent for months on end, so did she. She appears to have accepted his excuses for the prolonged silences—ill health, meetings, seminars, work, galleys—in exchange for one more declaration of his love and avowal of the trust that bound them. Twenty years later, however, Arendt said that Heidegger "lies notoriously always and everywhere, and whenever he can."[13] As she had had no contact with him since the early 1930s she could have been referring only to the time of their intimacy and probably to these excuses.

Heidegger let her believe that she could find happiness with another man while still loving him. At twenty-two Arendt was no match for the "fox," as she called him later.[14] He asked for photos of her to remind him of her sitting in his classroom, as though her departure was of little or no consequence. The lyrical stanzas bordering on kitsch, the lines trembling with passion, must have kept her uncertain and alert to his desire for her. Heidegger's language mirrors the change he underwent when reason gave way to passion. His first letters were written in a sophisticated, measured, well-crafted prose. His later letters disclose conventional sentimentality if not lowbrow taste; they possess the uninhibited language of unbridled emotion.

In early 1928 Heidegger made *his* decision. At an arranged meeting with Arendt in Heidelberg in April he told her that he no longer could continue the affair. At the beginning of the year his old teacher and steadfast champion Edmund Husserl had informed him confidentially that, after protracted deliberations and with Husserl's enthusiastic support, Heidegger was appointed full professor (*Ordinarius*) to the chair vacated by Husserl at Freiburg University. At the age of thirty-nine and with *Being and Time* just published, Heidegger was at the peak of his career. Perhaps he felt that the risk of discovery of his relationship with Arendt posed too great a personal danger. There was already another woman in the wings, however: Elisabeth Blochmann, "liebe Lisi," the half Jewish school friend of his wife, fourteen years older than Hannah, with an established academic career. In

1927 Heidegger had fondly thanked her for the "beautiful days in Berlin"; in 1928 he thanked her "for everything" and quoted Augustine's "volo ut sis" (I want you to be; *ich will, dass du seiest*) as he had three years before to Arendt.[15]

"That you will not come now—I think I have understood," Arendt wrote him toward the end of April 1928. The letter bore no salutation, a clear sign of the change that had occurred. She had been suffering, she told him, day in, day out since she had last seen him, from inexplicable sudden bouts of piercing angst. Heidegger, always the master of the situation, evidently had come to meet her with his mind made up, offering advice. "The road that you showed me," she wrote, "is longer and more difficult than I have thought. It takes up a whole, long life." But she was ready to follow this road of self-imposed solitude, as "this is the only possibility to live." To live meant for her to love him: "I would have lost my right to live had I lost my love for you," she wrote. For all its high drama, it is a desperate letter. Arendt's reluctance to speak openly about her feelings broke when he told her that he was leaving her. It must have taken all her willpower and courage to put these words on paper: "I love you, as I have the very first day—you know this, and I have always known this." Without the usual "your Hannah" (*Deine Hannah*), she ended the letter: " 'And with God's will / I will love you more after death' " (Arendt's quotes).[16]

Four

In September 1929 Hannah Arendt married Guenther Stern, another of Heidegger's students. Stern had earned his doctoral degree in philosophy under Husserl and proceeded to work on his habilitation thesis with Heidegger in Marburg, where in 1925 he met Hannah. He was a serious, gifted man with a fine sense of humor, but whatever his intentions at the time, Arendt paid him scant attention. However, a mere month after they met again at a New Year's party in Berlin in 1929, Arendt moved in with him. Theirs was a proper marriage, one that her mother and Stern's parents, pioneers in child psychology, greeted with joy. Arendt and Stern shared a common background, came from completely assimilated Jewish families, moved in the same circles, pursued similar intellectual goals, loved music and literature, and were devoted students of Heidegger's philosophy.

For all its propriety and good will on both sides, the marriage did not have much of a chance, since Hannah's love for Heidegger persisted. But Hannah Stern was a loyal wife and a devoted helpmate. She typed Stern's work, listened to page after page as he read aloud to her, offered advice, made suggestions, and retyped. They were good friends as long as the marriage lasted and remained on friendly terms after it was dissolved in 1937. It was Stern who in 1940 helped Arendt and Heinrich Bluecher obtain affidavits for emigration to the United States when they were forced to leave France (Stern and his parents had escaped to America earlier), and it was his sister who in the mid-1930s helped Arendt find a job in Paris with the Youth Alijah when unemployment threatened the very existence of the refugees. Decades later, Stern still spoke with respect and admiration for his first wife.

For two years the Sterns continued working: he on his habilitation thesis, leading to a university position, his ultimate goal, Hannah conducting research for a biography of Rahel Varnhagen. Stern wrote on the philosophy of music, but his work received no recognition from his professors, and he eventually abandoned it for journalism. At Jaspers's request Heidegger provided a letter of recommendation for Arendt to obtain a stipend. The financial help that her uncle from Berlin, Ernst Aron, had provided during her university studies (her mother, Martha Arendt Beerwald, and her husband were either unable to help, or Hannah felt more comfortable this way) was no longer available.

Although the Sterns lived on a shoestring following the 1929 stock market crash, they managed to maintain their rich social and cultural life. For some time they lived in Berlin; then they moved to Frankfurt and then back to Berlin, where Stern started his literary career under the pen name Guenther Anders. Fearing for his life as one of Bertolt Brecht's collaborators, Stern fled to Paris early in 1933, a move that ended the marriage as well.

In all likelihood, Martin Heidegger was a frequent topic of conversation for the Sterns (though Hannah kept her romantic involvement with him secret), and it was perhaps from

Guenther that Hannah learned about Heidegger's race prejudice. Stern remembered a long discussion with his mentor that left him convinced of Heidegger's "political reactionary tendencies and his fierce nationalism."[17] At another time, when he was invited to Heidegger's cabin in Todtnauberg with a group of students, Stern had left Heidegger "speechless" by standing on his head for five minutes, much longer than the other students. Heideger "seemed virtually insulted, because this was at odds with the negative picture he had of me," Stern recalled. That Stern could stand on his head at all, and then outlast the "big, blond darling pupils," was beyond the professor's comprehension. In the morning the whole group hiked back to Freiburg, Stern holding hands with Elfride Heidegger. Apparently unaware that he was a Jew, she suggested that he join the Nazis, whose physical fitness she admired. "Look at me," Stern retorted. "Then you'll see that I belong to those you wish to exclude."[18]

Despite her husband's experience, Arendt's feelings for Heidegger remained unchanged. In an undated letter probably written at the beginning of 1929, she told Heidegger that she had found "a haven from my restlessness and a sense of belonging with a man whom you would least understand"; and she recalled their last rendezvous in Heidelberg, which had strengthened anew her trust in him and left her happy. Meeting him again inspired her to "come to [him] today with the old sense of security and with the old request: do not forget me and do not forget how strongly and deeply I know that our love became the blessing of my life."

"I would like so much, so painfully, to know how you are, what you are working on, and how you like Freiburg," she continued. Unlike the letter of 22 April 1928, which ended with "And with God's will / I will love you more after death," this letter ended tenderly: "I kiss your brow and your eyes."[19]

Another undated letter was probably written in September or October 1929, after Arendt had married Guenther Stern. Heidegger paid a visit to the couple—possibly under the pretext of discussing Stern's habilitation thesis—and afterwards he and Stern took the same train, presumably to Freiburg. Arendt, wanting to catch a last glimpse of her lover, devised a scheme to appear secretly at the train station. In a letter she confessed her transgression; "forgive me," she implored him twice. In her imagination, she explained, she saw a picture of "you and Guenther" standing together at the train window, "and I alone at the platform." And that was exactly what had happened. Every time she saw him, she wrote, the past came rushing back, along with a renewed recognition that Heidegger provided "the continuity of my life, the continuity of our—*please* let me say this—love."

"I was standing in front of you for a few seconds, you actually saw me. You looked [at me] fleetingly. And, you did not recognize me." She felt invisible. A terrifying childhood memory gripped her, of a fairy tale her mother had read to her about a dwarf whose nose grew so big that no one could recognize him anymore. "My mother pretended as though this happened to me. I can still remember the blind fear when I kept crying: "But I'm really your child, I'm really Hannah," she wrote. "Today I felt the same way.

"And then the train rapidly rushed away. And it happened exactly as I have imagined: the two of you high up, above me, and I alone, utterly helpless. As always there was nothing I could do but let it happen, and wait, wait, wait."[20]

Not unlike Anna Karenina, hidden in the crowd at the train station, Hannah Arendt was observing her departing lover, unseen, unneeded.

Heidegger's last letter to Arendt until 1950—written, as its contents indicate, after he was appointed rector of Freiburg University, in the spring of 1933—responded to a letter from her in which she had conveyed distress over the rumor that he excluded Jews from his seminars, didn't greet his Jewish colleagues on the campus, rejected his Jewish doctoral students, and behaved like an antisemite. The word *Jew,* until then taboo, was finally put on paper, first by Arendt, then by Heidegger.

Heidegger vehemently and sarcastically denied the rumors. One by one he listed the favors he accorded to Jews—his accessibility to Jewish students, to whom he generously gave of his time, disruptive though it was to his own work, getting them stipends and discussing their dissertations with them. Who comes to him in an emergency? A Jew. Who insists on urgently discussing his doctoral degree? A Jew. Who sends him voluminous work for urgent critique?

A Jew. Who asks him for help in obtaining grants? Jews. For whom did he arrange a stipend in Rome? A Jew. If anyone brands this kind of behavior antisemitic, so be it, he said. He is as much an antisemite today as he was twenty years before and in Marburg—a not very subtle allusion to his affair with Arendt. In other words, he was saying, were I an antisemite would I have loved you?

Of course, he complained, he had been slandered all through his career, so how could he expect any gratitude from his students, including Arendt. To further confuse the angry and not quite logical argument, Heidegger insisted that all the talk about his alleged antisemitism had nothing to do with his personal relationships with Jews, and he mentioned some Jewish scholars, among them Husserl. And certainly antisemitism could in no way affect his attitude toward her.

How did Arendt react to this letter? Was Heidegger indeed a victim of slander? Or did she see that he drew a distinct line between Germans and German Jews, between himself and the German Jews, his colleagues and students, to whom he accorded special favors. This division involved them both: not a woman and a man, but a Jewess and a German.

Had she been aware that in October 1929 Heidegger had written a letter in which he cautioned a high official in the Ministry of Education against the "growing Judaisation" (*Verjudung*), his posture would not have come as a surprise to her. Heidegger wrote: "[T]he matter concerns no less than an urgent recognition that we are confronted with a choice—either we will replenish our *German* spiritual life with genuine native forces and educators or we will once and for all surrender it to the growing Judaisation in a broader and narrower sense."[21] Arendt was, after all, one of the future scholars who, in Heidegger's view, "Judaised" the souls of German youth. But she had not read the letter. It was discovered in 1989.

One can only speculate about her reflections, which she of course did not share with anyone. Arendt idealized Heidegger beyond measure, so it is not impossible that she brushed away the thought that the man she seemed to know so well might be involved in unsavory practices. A time was to come when she would call Heidegger a "potential murderer," blaming him for precipitating Husserl's death. But that time was far away, and she would eventually take back her words.

It is conceivable that Heidegger's ambivalent letter to her, along with the news about his pro-Hitler Rectorial Address and his joining the National Socialist Party, sealed Arendt's decision to leave Germany in August 1933.

It took ten years for Arendt to gain enough confidence to disavow the promise she had made to herself "never to love a man again." In Paris in 1936 she met Heinrich Bluecher, a German refugee like herself. When she was away on a personal or business trip they corresponded regularly (sometimes daily), and her first letters to him reveal the insecurity that the affair with Heidegger had instilled in her. She wouldn't put a salutation on a letter, even after Bluecher opened his with "My dearest." Nor would she end a letter with more than her initial. Worried about the lack of news from him—the precarious existence of "enemy aliens" in France justified her concern—she asked him merely to confirm the receipt of her letters. "This *in no way* obligates you to write," she emphasized somewhat comically. "Only to confirm!"[22] Always, she left it to him to make the first move. "It was really stupid of me to forget to confirm your letters. I received all of them and 'confirm' the receipt with all my heart," Bluecher teased her.[23] "I thought you didn't like my letter," Arendt wrote, "and that's why you didn't write."[24] Only after Bluecher wrote, "Dearest, I love you," did she respond with a qualified "dearest, I think, I love you."[25]

In the years that had gone by Arendt certainly gave much thought to her affair with Heidegger, which, in a sense, was not finished. Heidegger loved her, she believed, but he humiliated her, relentlessly maneuvered her into one box or another, so that all she could do was "wait, wait, wait." At the age of thirty, a bundle of inhibitions and fears, she mistrusted her own feelings and Bluecher's as well. She inched her way into the new relationship with utmost caution, suspiciously and uncertainly.

The friendship, the strongest bond in their relationship, developed in spite of Arendt's reserve and because of Bluecher's stubborn belief that they belonged together. They were two shipwrecked people who had left behind their country, friends, families, work, dreams. Their dreams were entirely different: Hannah, totally apolitical, was working her way up to an academic career; Bluecher, a proletarian with no formal education, fought, gun in hand, in the ranks of the extreme leftist Spartacus and later joined the German Communist Party. She became a refugee because she was a Jew, he because he was a communist. Both brought their nightmares into exile, and the nightmares brought them close.

Shattered by yet another roundup of his comrades in Germany, Bluecher described in a letter to Arendt a recurrent dream "because I promised to tell you everything."[26] In the dream he saw executioners, tortures, long knives, breathless flights through murky buildings, and he relived his attempts to escape the Gestapo, to save a trapped friend. Bluecher's horror, compounded by having to abandon his friends, haunted his days as well. Arendt understood that by sharing his torment and guilt with her he was telling her that they were bound by an affinity far beyond attraction or affection. And she responded. In a letter bearing the salutation, "My dear friend," she wrote: "You forced me to trust you, but only you, and only between the two of us."[27]

Toward the end of August 1936, after they had been seeing each other for about three months, Arendt was almost ready to commit herself: "That I love you—you knew already in Paris, as I did," she wrote from Switzerland. "If I didn't say it, it was because I was afraid of the consequences. And what I can say today is only: we shall try—for the sake of our love. Whether I can be your wife, whether I will, I do not know."[28]

In his letters Bluecher was warm but not sentimental, wise but not overpowering or patronizing, respectful of Arendt's mind and independence, caring but not possessive or domineering. "I have never known what it means to belong unconditionally to another person," she wrote him. And two days later: "I feel so secure in your love. . . . And I love you deeply, impetuously, and fondly."[29]

After Heidegger's suffocating, cagy, and often ponderous letters, Bluecher's were a breath of fresh air. Attentive to her spiritual and physical well-being, unafraid of getting involved in every sphere of her life, he assumed responsibility for her in an unobtrusive, natural way. He gave her the freedom to be weak, insecure, and afraid. When Arendt went to see her mother in Switzerland, he wrote that everything that concerned her was important to him—her relationship with her mother (which was not free from tension, he knew), and her work, diet, rest, and warmth. He insisted repeatedly in his letters that Hannah buy a warm winter coat for herself, until she gave in and did so.

Arendt probably recoiled from drawing any comparison between Heidegger and Bluecher or the love each gave her. But after several years and living in exile, she saw herself with different eyes. "When I met you," she wrote Bluecher, "I finally wasn't afraid anymore, after the initial shock which actually was still a child's shock played out in adulthood."[30] The fear that had first gripped her when she was a child was not assuaged by Martin Heidegger. If anything, it intensified during Arendt's affair with him.

It took her time to get used to the idea that she could have both love and her own identity, since for years she had had to barter one for the other and live constantly at odds with herself. Bluecher showed her that such a compromise was incompatible with either love or friendship. "Finally," she said, "I know what happiness actually is."[31] Slowly she learned that love in itself, no matter how passionate, can be destructive if it is isolated from the realities of life and based solely on sexual drive and the exercise of power. It certainly was for her.

Significantly, in her pre-war correspondence with Bluecher she never mentioned Heidegger's name, but it was not difficult for Bluecher to realize that she was a woman afraid of emotional intimacy and rejection. He would poke fun at her, gently, for inserting the qualifying "I think" before "I love you," betraying less her uncertainty than her fear of expressing commitment.[32] To Heidegger she had said "I love you," thus surrendering her independence. Now she waited. Still, when she told Bluecher, "If I cannot exist as I, if the price I pay for love is my independence," he certainly drew his own conclusions about her experiences.[33] Yet even after Arendt told him about her youthful romance (probably after the war, when Heidegger stood accused of Nazism), Bluecher, commonsensical and revolted by the peculiarly German sentimental suffering, never fully understood, as their postwar letters make clear, the depth of her bond with the philosopher. He erroneously considered her affair with Heidegger as ended.

Bluecher understood love as a galvanizing physical and spiritual force that required the partners to leave open spaces for each other to develop, act, and create. "You will be who you are," he wrote Arendt in September 1937. "And so will I." Independence and dependence, inseparable, were a source of strength for both. And so was erotic pleasure. "So, I have changed you from a girl into a woman? How wonderful."[34]

Not even the security of Bluecher's love entirely restored Arendt's self-confidence. In 1937, when they already were living together—Arendt was in no rush to get married—she wrote to him in Paris from Geneva: "See, Heinrich, at the beginning I wrote every other day because I wasn't quite sure of your reaction and because in such matters I follow you—almost slavishly. Because—and this is a woman's eternal fear—a woman is always afraid of having her love, or the overabundance of her love, perceived as a burden."[35]

Ten years after Heidegger requested that she not write to him without his permission she was still half paralyzed. Though women were conditioned to react rather than act, Heidegger reinforced the "slavish" streak in her. An independent and unconventional woman, Arendt still saw men, in personal life, in their traditional role.

Hannah Arendt severed her ties with Martin Heidegger when she left Germany. Karl Jaspers, Arendt's mentor, maintained his friendship with Heidegger until Heidegger himself put an end to it. Both Arendt and Jaspers initiated a conciliation after the war, and though their reasons for making the first step were as different as their ties to Heidegger, the underlying cause was the same: the power Heidegger exercised over them.

Jaspers considered Heidegger his only peer in the realm of philosophy. They met in 1920 in the house of Edmund Husserl. There was an instant mutual understanding between the widely recognized professor and the young lecturer. A friendship developed, based on their shared approach to philosophy and dissatisfaction with "academic philosophy." The relationship continued even after Heidegger embraced National Socialism in 1933; it was cut short by Heidegger in 1936. When their link was resumed by Jaspers's 1949 letter it was a shadow of the former bond. Jaspers's letters to Heidegger are evidence of the constant inner struggle Jaspers fought not so much because Heidegger abandoned him but because he genuinely wanted Heidegger back in his life. Just as Arendt evoked their shared past in her postwar letters to Heidegger, the seventy-year-old Jaspers wrote to Heidegger in 1953: "I see you before me, as though it were just now," recalling Heidegger's frequent visits with him.[36]

It was a complicated affair throughout, just as was

Arendt's with Heidegger. Arendt and Jaspers were both attracted to Heidegger and both struggled, for different reasons but equally unsuccessfully, against this attraction: he was a force they could not resist. "Poor Heidegger," Jaspers said to Arendt in 1949, on her first visit to him after the war. "[H]ere we are sitting, the two best friends he has, and we see right through him."[37] They saw through Heidegger's duplicity, hypocrisy, manipulations, yet this did not deter either of them from trying to repair the broken ties.

Arendt did not tell Jaspers that she had thought of seeing Heidegger on the same trip. She wanted to spare her friend's feelings and probably was not sure herself whether she would make the visit to Heidegger, something she had agonized over for a long time. She knew that Jaspers would be pained by the renewal of her contact with Heidegger, though she could hardly have known that Jaspers was fighting his own desire to see Heidegger. Unaware of Jaspers's personal drama, she attributed Jaspers's grudge to Heidegger's collaboration with the Nazis. In March 1951, a year after she finally met with Heidegger, she assured Jaspers that Heidegger "really does not know and is hardly in a position to find out what devil had then possessed him," an explanation Jaspers ignored.[38] Over the years Heidegger would implore Arendt to intercede and bring about a reconciliation between him and Jaspers. It seems, however, that the restored ties between Arendt and Heidegger in fact made Jaspers more uneasy if not envious and helped further estrange him from Heidegger. In 1949 the men exchanged fourteen letters and in 1950, eight; from 1952 to 1963 five letters are extant. Arendt intervened many times with Jaspers on Heidegger's behalf, as she informed her husband, to no avail.* Three years before he died, Jaspers, eager for Arendt to understand that there was more than one Heidegger, shed some light on his feelings about him.

From 1928 to 1964 Jaspers made notes to himself about Heidegger's work, character, and behavior, and, significantly, he wrote down his thoughts about Heidegger and his philosophy. As his friend and assistant Hans Saner reports, the notes were found on his desk after he died in 1969 and published by Saner in 1978.[39] Jaspers wrote a chapter about Heidegger and their friendship in the mid-1950s for his *Philosophical Autobiography* but after long deliberation left it out (it was first included in the 1977 edition), knowing that Heidegger would be "mortally wounded" and not wanting to risk a final break.[40] From the beginning the friendship was meant to be a forum through which they could "do philosophy" together and form a philosophical comrade-in-arms combat union of two (*Kampfgemeinschaft*). Almost from the beginning the friendship was strained.

Twenty years later Jaspers admitted to himself that he had heard early on "falsely sounding tunes." In 1924 Heidegger had characterized Jaspers's essay "The Idea of the Univer-

*Hannah Arendt wrote to Bluecher on 24 May 1952: "This thing with Jaspers was a terrible blow to him [Heidegger]. He does suffer because of it, and I myself am rather unhappy that I cannot do anything. . . . I will see Jaspers next week, but it is quite hopeless." LC.

sity" as "the most trivial of trivialities." Confronted by Jaspers, Heidegger denied having ever made such a statement. Jaspers responded, "Then the matter is for me nonexistent and finished," much to Heidegger's surprise, as Jaspers recalls.[41] Jaspers accepted any glaring lie, as did Arendt, rather than lose Heidegger. Even an alarm bell failed to shake his confidence in Heidegger. In 1923 Heidegger wrote to Jaspers: "You certainly know that Husserl was appointed to a chair at the Berlin University; he behaves worse than an instructor. . . . Husserl is entirely out of joint—if he ever was 'in'—which recently became increasingly questionable to me; he shifts backwards and forwards and delivers himself of such trivialities that can evoke only pity. He lives for his mission of 'the founder of phenomenology,' but no one knows what that actually is."[42] So eager was Jaspers to nurture the budding friendship with his junior colleague, and so uncritical, that he let this crude act of disloyalty pass without comment. Ten years later Heidegger would dispose of Jaspers as he had of Husserl. Yet on the occasion of Husserl's seventieth birthday, in 1929, Heidegger effusively lauded his teacher for creating a new philosophy and new ways of thinking, and for changing the entire outlook of Western philosophy. In another four years Husserl would receive a circular letter signed by Rector Heidegger forbidding him to enter the university premises.

Heidegger "was the only one among my friends with whom I disagreed in 1933, the only one who betrayed me," Jaspers wrote in his notes.[43] If he disagreed with Heidegger, Jaspers kept it to himself, as his letter of 23 August 1933, congratulating Heidegger on his (infamous) Rectorial Address, and subsequent letters indicate. During his visit in June 1933, which turned out to be the last time the two would meet, Jaspers confessed that his Jewish wife, Gertrud, cried over the news she read in the newspapers. Heidegger responded, "It makes one feel better to cry sometimes," and left without properly taking his leave from Mrs. Jaspers, in whose house he had stayed for long stretches dating back to 1920.[44] To Jaspers's question "How can a man as coarse as Hitler govern Germany?" Heidegger replied in all seriousness: "Culture is of no importance. Just look at his marvelous hands." Told by Jaspers about the "vicious nonsense," the "Protocols of the Elders of Zion," Heidegger said: "But the dangerous international alliance of the Jews still exists."[45] All this did not deter Jaspers from inviting Heidegger to his house: "If it were possible for you to come again to Heidelberg in October [1933] I would be very pleased. . . . It's a pleasure for me to speak with you." Further, Jaspers praised the "extraordinary step" taken by the government to modify radically the governance of universities. Accordingly, the rector became the university's "Fuehrer," with all the rights of the former senate vested in him; he was no longer to be elected but appointed by the minister. The senate was to act in an advisory capacity, and the deans were to be appointed by the rector. "Since I know from my own experience," Jaspers continues, "how the present [university] constitution works . . . I cannot but find the new constitution right." The total subjugation of the university to the National Socialist government was a step in the right direction, Jaspers thought, though some further changes, which he suggested to Heidegger, were still required. "I wish this aristocratic principle full success," he wrote with undisguised eagerness.[46] Jaspers not only accepted the miniature totalitarian state in the guise of the university but he also greeted it with enthusiasm. On account of his Jewish wife Jaspers was excluded from participation in university management in 1933, and he lost his chair in 1937. After 1937 his works were no longer published in Germany.* All of these events were met by silence from Heidegger.

Jaspers, like Arendt, readily acknowledged Heidegger's superiority. "Philosophy in German universities lies in all probability in your hands for a long time to come," he wrote to Heidegger in 1931. "As long as I live," he acknowledged "with deep pain," "I will be able to work with pen and paper only." Jaspers's homage and his humble admission that Heidegger was his "only colleague who knew what I had *not* accomplished" were seen by Heidegger as signs of weakness rather than of strength and trust.[47] He was to bring this home to Jaspers more than once, but he trusted him enough to submit Jaspers's name to the Freiburg University Verification Commission to speak in his defense after the war. Jaspers did so to the best of his abilities: he was not as forthcoming as he could have been.

*In 1939 Jaspers turned down the invitation of the Caisse Nationale de la Recherche Scientifique in Paris, which was extended to enable him to leave Germany.

Jaspers's postwar correspondence with Heidegger shows how desperately he wanted to believe in Heidegger's decency and honesty, in spite of their sharp political differences. On 7 March 1950, Heidegger wrote to Jaspers, "I haven't come to your house since 1933 not because a Jewish woman lived there but *because I was simply ashamed*."[48] "I thank you warmly for your candid explanation," Jaspers responded, though he later called Heidegger's explanation an "excuse." "It means a great deal to me that you said frankly you were 'ashamed.'"[49] Heidegger wrote in the same letter: "At the end of the thirties . . . I thought immediately about your wife. I received then from Professor Wilser a firm assurance that nothing would happen to your wife." (Julius Wilser was chancellor at Freiburg during Heidegger's tenure as rector.) Apparently Heidegger was unaware that Gertrud Jaspers was twice in mortal danger and had to go into hiding to escape deportation. Still, Jaspers chose to believe the unbelievable, as did Arendt, whom Heidegger convinced in 1950 that he was a helpless victim of malicious slander. "I thank you for your concern in 1939 and for your intervention through Wilser. You did think of us," Jaspers wrote with evident relief, forgetting that Heidegger did not utter a word when Jaspers was barred from teaching and publishing. "You will forgive me when I tell you what I had sometimes thought: that you seemed to behave with regard to the national-socialist events like a boy who dreams, does not know what he is doing . . . and soon stands helpless facing a heap of rubble and lets himself be driven even deeper."[50] A boy (*ein Knabe*), dreaming, helpless, innocent. The boyish, innocent dreamer was Jaspers, not Heidegger.

Hannah Arendt also described Heidegger, in a letter to her husband, as "defenseless" and "helpless."[51]

Martin Heidegger's two best friends concealed from the world at large their intimate knowledge of him. Arendt and Jaspers were seriously involved in questions of ethics and morality, but their theories failed them when it came to Martin Heidegger.

Seven

The cases of Heidegger's other students, Eduard Baumgarten and Max Mueller, and of Professor Hermann Staudinger are relevant to the understanding of Heidegger the man—not the philosopher or member of the National Socialist Party or educator—and thereby his relationship with Hannah Arendt. Neither his philosophy nor political affiliation but his principles and inner convictions prompted his actions. A true believer in the spiritual mission of the superior German Aryan race, he set out, as Adolf Hitler put it in *Mein Kampf,* to "recover" what his opponents "in their criminal stupidity" let go to waste.[52]

Heidegger's treatment of Baumgarten, his doctoral student and assistant designate, finally jolted Jaspers out of his relative complacency. In 1934 or 1935, Marianne Weber, the widow of the German sociologist and political economist Max Weber, gave Jaspers a copy of a confidential report Heidegger wrote in 1933 for the attention of the League of National Socialist University Lecturers in Goettingen in order to block Baumgarten's promotion. Baumgarten, he wrote, "was at least here [University of Freiburg] anything but a National Socialist. By family ties and spiritual disposition he is an heir to the liberal-democratic Heidelberg intellectual circle of Max Weber. After he had failed me, he became closely tied to the Jew Fraenkel, formerly employed at Goettingen, and now dismissed from this university."[53]

Eduard Fraenkel was until the summer semester of 1933 a

professor of classic philology at the University of Freiburg; he was in exile a professor at Oxford from 1935. Jaspers's profound shock is expressed in his testimonial, written in 1945 at the request of the Freiburg University Verification Commission. Unaware that Jaspers possessed the compromising document, and counting on the old ties of friendship, Heidegger himself chose Jaspers to address the question of his alleged antisemitism.

"In the twenties Heidegger was not an antisemite," Jaspers stated, unaware of Heidegger's 1929 "Judaisation" letter and his open dismay at the large number of Jewish medical students. "This completely unnecessary word about the Jew Fraenkel proves that in 1933 he became an antisemite, at least in certain cases."[54] Jaspers also wrote that Heidegger and a number of other professors attempted to become spiritual leaders of the National Socialist movement. By placing Heidegger among "different professors," none of whom equaled him in prominence or in aspiring to become Adolf Hitler's leading ideologue, Jaspers, it seems, tried to minimize Heidegger's subservience to Nazi ideology as well as his prodigious ambition.

Max Mueller, after 1946 a professor of philosophy at the University of Freiburg, was, in his own words, one of Heidegger's "favorite pupils."[55] In 1937 he was denounced to the authorities because of his affiliation with a Catholic student group. The vice rector, Theodor Maunz, warned Mueller that Heidegger, when requested to submit his opinion on Mueller's political convictions, praised him as a scholar and educator but criticized Mueller's negative attitude toward Nazi Germany. Maunz encouraged Mueller to ask Heidegger to delete the one phrase that hurt Mueller's chances to obtain a university position. Heidegger refused. He told the desperate young scholar that he wrote "the only answer that corresponds with the truth," though he "packaged" it neatly. Mueller pleaded with his teacher to reconsider and remove the incriminating sentence. Heidegger answered, not without sarcasm: "As a Catholic, you should know that one must tell the truth. Therefore I can not delete the sentence. . . . There is nothing I can do. Do not hold it against me." "My last words," Mueller recalled, "were, 'The point is not that I might hold it against you. The point is that my very existence depends on it.'" Subsequently he was informed that for "ideological and political reasons" he was unacceptable to Berlin University.[56]

Hermann Staudinger, who was awarded the Nobel Prize in chemistry in 1953, held a teaching position in Zurich during the First World War. A pacifist and antinationalist, he obtained Swiss citizenship in 1920, though he retained German citizenship as well. His dossier, which contained documents accusing Staudinger of advising enemy countries on the production of materiels essential to chemical warfare, was kept in the German Consulate General in Zurich. In July 1933, according to Hugo Ott, Heidegger dispatched to Zurich an instructor in physics, Dr. Alfons Buehl, to collect information on Staudinger, then a professor of chemistry at Freiburg. The German ambassador to Switzerland, Ernst

Freiherr von Weizsaecker, sent the required documents to the Foreign Office around Christmas 1933. The Ministry of Culture and the Gestapo turned to Rector Heidegger in February 1934 for information concerning Staudinger. Heidegger was already in possession of the documents, obtained at his own initiative, so his report on Staudinger was ready in just four days. Significantly, Heidegger wrote the report *after* he decided, on 1 January 1934, according to his 1945 deposition, to resign the rectorship. In the report he reiterated the accusation that Staudinger collaborated in wartime with Germany's enemies, noting that "in January 1917, at the time the Fatherland was in grave danger, St[audinger] applied for Swiss citizenship." Most incriminating, in Heidegger's view, was Staudinger's open admission of his "firm opposition toward the national currents in Germany and his repeated statements that he would never carry arms in support of the Fatherland." Heidegger recommended "dismissal rather than retirement." (Ironically, the verdict of the Ministry of Culture, which was to discredit Staudinger as an "educator of the German university youth," was identical to that passed on Heidegger after the Second World War.) However, afraid of worldwide repercussions, the authorities did not follow Heidegger's recommendation, and the famous chemist retained his position. [57]

What motivated Heidegger to start his own investigation into Staudinger's past? In view of Heidegger's persistent protestations that he agreed to assume the rectorship reluctantly "in the interests of the university," to protect it from the Party's interference, and that he joined the Party (was "ordered" to join it, in his words) for the same reason, the initiative he took seems inexplicable and casts doubt on his veracity.[58] Hermann Staudinger was one of the most illustrious scholars on the faculty at Freiburg. He was not a Catholic, not a liberal or social democrat, not a Jew, but a pacifist and antinationalist. Heidegger's revulsion against a German who displayed such sentiments evidently led him to believe that Staudinger, apart from deserving the harshest punishment, should have no access to students, not even in a chemistry laboratory. Hugo Ott maintains that had the "case Staudinger" been known while the "case Heidegger" was pending after 1945, "Heidegger would not have had the slightest chance to be rehabilitated."[59]

Baumgarten was politically unreliable because of his former association with liberal intellectuals and with Professor Fraenkel, a Jew. In addition, he had taught at the University of Wisconsin and written his habilitation thesis on John Dewey and thus was contaminated by American pragmatism and materialism. Mueller was a practicing Catholic and, in Heidegger's eyes, an enemy of the regime, unfit to educate young Germans. Staudinger offended Heidegger's nationalism and his cult of the German warrior.

An early enthusiast of National Socialism, Elfride Heidegger fully supported her husband's efforts to help it fasten its grip on the country, especially on its youth. The Heideggers were united in the belief that only "radical change" (*Umwaelzung,* Hitler's favorite expression, frequently used by Martin Heidegger) could "rejuvenate" Germany and restore its political and spiritual leadership in the world. Their shared belief provided an additional bond between them, a fact entirely unappreciated by Hannah Arendt. Though Arendt called the marriage a "classic case of the mob-elite bond," Elfride was perhaps an ideal wife for Heidegger.[60] When they married, the young instructor had no money and no permanent job, and there was no indication of the prominence he was to achieve. She stood firmly by him during the two most critical times in his life: the break with the Catholic Church and Germany's defeat, which left him stripped of position, status, and prestige, albeit temporarily. Heidegger's apologists (including Hannah Arendt) endeavored to portray him as a helpless victim of her sinister obsession, and to show her as the dark force who urged him to join the Nazis, ruined his life, and was the cause of all his misfortunes. It was an easy way to absolve him of responsibility for his own decisions, except it was not true. Whatever Heidegger was, he was never a tool in the hands of his wife or anyone else.

Heidegger was extremely proud of his wife's achievements as an educator of girl students. He repeatedly informed Elisabeth Blochmann, the half Jewish friend who was tutoring German at Oxford after being fired from her job, about his wife's activities and accomplishments: "Elfride is very well," he wrote her in 1937. "She is surrounded by a delightful circle of female students with whom she works."[61] Frau Heidegger strove for equal access to education for women at all levels, evoking the teachings of Hitler and his concept of women as "comrades of the people." She stressed the importance of preserving the purity of the Aryan race and defending it against the corrosive influence of the Jews and Communists. Her Party activities did not cease, as Heidegger claimed his did, after her husband's resignation in 1934. This caused no disagreements between them nor did it diminish Heidegger's respect for her work. She continued teaching about women's rights until her workers were reduced to digging trenches. Elfride Heidegger "brutalized in the worst possible way" the women workers under her command, refusing to exempt from labor "the sick and the pregnant" during the bitter winter of 1944.[62]

Elfride Heidegger often accompanied her husband on official trips. In September 1933 she went with him to Berlin. "It is wonderful that Elfride will be with you during these decisive days," wrote Elisabeth Blochmann.[63] In 1936 the Heideggers traveled together to Rome, where Heidegger delivered a lecture in the Italian-German Cultural Institute. There he met privately with his former student Karl Loewith, who remembered that Heidegger's "wife greeted me with a mixture of stiff and friendly reserve"—Loewith used to take care of the Heidegger boys, so Elfride was well acquainted with him—and Heidegger promptly "steered her clear from alluding to the situation in Germany and his own attitude toward it."[64] Though the swastika pin was prominently displayed in his lapel, Heidegger apparently thought it prudent not to let his wife exhibit her elation over the Nazis to Loewith, now a refugee, owing to his half Jewish origin.

A kindred spirit in the political realm and an authority of sorts because of her Prussian military background, Elfride occupied an increasingly influential role in her husband's life. With friends, colleagues, and students dismissed, exiled, pensioned, shunned, Heidegger needed her more than ever. And he was foremost on her mind as well. When they were younger and money was scarce and the future uncertain, she had the cabin in Todtnauberg built for him to give him space to think and let him be closer to nature, an elemental need of his. Now, not always comfortable with the regime's policies, he could lean on a wife who had no doubts or scruples but an unwavering faith in Adolf Hitler, and who supported her husband in the conviction that they were on the right side.

Elfride Heidegger was a woman of independent mind, great vitality, and considerable inner resources. She neither idolized nor underestimated her husband; she respected him and demanded respect in return. In the early postwar years, with both sons prisoners of war in the Soviet Union and her husband demoralized, she showed resilience. She fought ferociously to retrieve their house and his library, which had been sequestrated by the French military authorities (who declared him a *nazi typique*), so that he could continue to work.[65] It is conceivable that, in view of his poor mental state, she coauthored the statement covering his Nazi past that Heidegger presented in November 1945 to the rector of the University of Freiburg. The document repeats the arguments that she had used in order to recover their house: that after 1933 Heidegger had abandoned the Nazi credo and devoted himself exclusively to philosophy and teaching; that there was a ban imposed on the publication of his books and on foreign travel; that he was an apolitical, unworldly, harmless scholar who, driven by the honorable goal to save the university, became a target of Nazi persecution.

It was she who refused to accept help from friends willing to intervene with the French and the Vatican in order to obtain information about their sons. It was he who, out of her hearing, asked for help.* It was she who finally got back their house and, with her usual care, restored his study and the cabin in Todtnauberg. He was strong, she knew, and would ultimately persevere, but she also knew how much he depended on her trust in his judgment and beliefs, which time did nothing to change. The temporary setback did not undermine his fundamental faith in the German people: they lost nothing of their primeval values, which would sustain them no matter how long the night.

*Hugo Ott kindly shared this information with me. See also Ott, *Martin Heidegger, Unterwegs zu seiner Biographie,* 158.

Heidegger never underestimated his wife in his private or his public life. His only remorse about his affair with Hannah Arendt, he told Hannah in 1950, was that he had cheated on his wife instead of telling her the truth at once, which she would have understood and accepted for the sake of his happiness. Elfride Heidegger's appreciation of his need for solitude (or of company, as the case might be) and her willingness to leave him alone while shouldering the burdens of everyday life and raising the children herself impressed him. She had no intellectual ambitions nor did she pretend to have any, but she was intelligent enough to comprehend the difference between her husband's mind and her own, and this he appreciated as well. He reconciled himself to her refusal to accompany him to Messkirch to visit friends and family, foremost his beloved brother Fritz. He probably attributed the estrangement to his humble background and her elevated one.

Until 1950, Hannah Arendt did not know Elfride Heidegger. Nor did she know anything about the couple's life or Heidegger's attitude toward his wife. These were not topics Heidegger discussed with her. Because he loved her, Arendt might have imagined that he was unhappily married; she was too young to understand the difference between a wife and a mistress in a man's life. When she came to know Heidegger's wife, if only superficially, Arendt's opinion of her grew from bad to worse, although Heidegger made it clear that he loved and needed his wife. Naturally the women were jealous of each other. Heidegger, at least on the surface, wanted his wife and his former mistress to become close friends, but it seems that in reality he rather enjoyed being the object of both women's attentions. In any case, Arendt never ceased to believe that she was *the* woman in Heidegger's life.

The end of the war found Heidegger in Messkirch. He had fled by bicycle from bombed Freiburg, to which he had returned after a spell in the *Volkssturm,* the German territorial army. Drafting him was, Heidegger claimed in his statement to the rector of Freiburg University, the Party's final act of persecution, although all men between sixteen and sixty (he was fifty-six) able to carry arms were mobilized in the last effort to save the Third Reich.

In June 1945, Prince Bernhard von Sachsen-Meiningen and his wife, Margot, invited a small circle of friends to a piano concert and a lecture by Professor Martin Heidegger. This was to be Heidegger's next to last semi-official public appearance (he gave several lectures in Bremen in 1949) before the ban on his teaching was lifted in 1950.[66]

Heidegger devoted himself, with the help of his wife, not so much to defending or justifying his twelve-year record in Nazi Germany as to reinterpreting, rewriting, and reinventing that period in his life. Together they worked to convert the accusations against him into the truth as he saw it: to present himself as an opponent of the regime, a fighter against communism, a savior of Western civilization, a leader of spiritual resistance. To convince the world philosophic community that he was being victimized first by the vanquished and later by the conquerors was a formidable job.

Heidegger wanted not only to transform his past, he also wanted praise, admiration, and recognition for the suffering to which he claimed the Nazis had subjected him. The hearing before the Verification Commission and his statement were designed to set the record straight: yes, he had supported the NS regime in the early years, but only because the Western world was threatened by Communism; yes, he had believed that Hitler stood on behalf of *the whole Volk* for renewal, and this was his mistake; yes, he had accepted the Social and National principles—though not National Socialism—because as he saw it the Social and National were not intrinsically connected to biological racist theory; no, he had never read *Mein Kampf* through because of his "opposition to its contents"; yes, he had failed to attend Husserl's funeral, but he had been bedridden.[67]

For his resistance—"resistance" and "spiritual resistance" appear frequently throughout the statement—he was punished by being banned from scholarly conferences and lecturing abroad (he was in Rome in 1936 and in Zurich in 1935–36; according to Ott, invitations from Spain, Portugal, and Italy extended to Heidegger in 1942 were officially approved and accepted by him but did not materialize because of conflicts in his schedule); by a ban on his publications (*Being and Time* was reissued in 1936 and 1942); and by being "constantly watched" by spies—he came up with the name of one student, killed in the war, who he said confessed to him that he was an informer.[68] He emphasized his contribution to the education of "young men and (too many) women students" in whom, between 1934 and 1944, he instilled Western spiritual values, mindless of the danger he courted by doing so. The closing statement reads: "When Husserl died I was sick, in bed. Admittedly after recovering I did not write to Mrs. Husserl, which was doubtless a failure on my part; the reason behind it was painful shame over what was meantime . . . done to the Jews and that one ["one," in German "*man*," is an impersonal pronoun, here used to avoid the personal pronoun "I"] was helpless when confronted with it."[69]

The *apologia pro vita sua*, running to almost six single-spaced pages, is a masterpiece. By presenting himself as a victim, Heidegger included himself among the countless millions the Nazis had destroyed. He was always attuned to the mood of his people: when he joined the ranks of the Nazis and when he passed himself off as a victim—of the Nazis *and* of the Allies. In each case he emerged triumphant, unrepentant, unyielding, unremorseful. He did not recant, he did not retract, nor did he ever publicly (or privately, as to Hannah Arendt or Karl Jaspers) condemn the Nazi atrocities. He did not, Jaspers thought, undergo any change, because he—"my spiritual enemy"—was incapable of grasping the depth of his failure as a human being.[70]

The protracted denazification took a heavy toll on Heidegger. In the spring of 1946, suffering from physical and mental collapse, he underwent treatment in a sanatorium. Heidegger, evidently in despair, turned to Archbishop Conrad Groeber, who had taken the fourteen-year-old Heidegger, the future Catholic theologian, under his wing. Groeber wrote to the German political adviser to Pope Pius XII: "It was a considerable comfort for me when, at the beginning of his misfortune, he [Heidegger] came to me and conducted himself in a genuinely edifying manner. I told him the whole truth and he accepted it, in tears. I will not break off my relations with him because I hope for his spiritual transformation."[71] The hope of the archbishop remained unfulfilled.

Hannah Arendt first mentioned Heidegger's name in print in "What Is Existenz Philosophy?" published in *Partisan Review* in 1946. In a footnote* she observed that Heidegger "forbade Husserl, his teacher and friend, whose lecture chair he had inherited, to enter the faculty, because Husserl was a Jew."[72] Karl Jaspers, with whom she carried on a regular correspondence, objected: "The remark about Heidegger is actually not exact."[73] He assumed, he explained, that Arendt had referred to a circular letter which every rector had to write to professors dismissed on the government's orders. Arendt responded that in her opinion Heidegger should have resigned rather than sign such a letter. "And because I know," she wrote, "that this letter and this signature almost killed him [Husserl], I cannot but regard Heidegger as a potential murderer." Arendt was well informed about the interviews Heidegger granted, in which he touched on his cooperation with the Nazis and the overtures he made to the French philosophers: "Nothing but foolish lies with, it seems to me, a pronounced pathological streak. But," she added, clearly referring to her personal experience, "that's an old story."[74]

*Incidentally, in the same footnote Arendt referred to Heidegger as the "last (we hope) romantic." The quotation, taken out of context, has often been distorted to infer Arendt's nostalgia rather than sarcasm.

In a 1949 letter to Jaspers, Arendt wrote:

Heidegger. . . . What you call impurity, I'd call lack of character, but in the sense that he has literally none, certainly not an especially bad one. . . . I read the letter against humanism [Martin Heidegger, "Ueber den Humanismus," Letter to Jean Beaufret, Bern, 1947], also very questionable and much too often ambiguous, yet still the first thing he wrote that is up to his old standard. (I have read here [Heidegger's work] about Hoelderlin, and the absolutely horrible, chatty lectures on Nietzsche.) That life in Todtnauberg, this railing against civilization, and writing Sein with a y is in reality a kind of mouse hole into which he withdrew, assuming with good reason that the only people he will have to see are pilgrims filled with admiration for him; no one is likely to climb 1200 meters just to make a scene. And even if someone did just that, then he will lie through his teeth and hope to God that nobody will call him a liar to his face. He certainly believed that by using this stratagem he could buy off the whole world at the lowest possible price and cheat his way out of everything that is embarrassing to him, and then do nothing but philosophize.[75]

The next time Arendt wrote to Jaspers about Heidegger, in March 1951, she tried to justify Heidegger's wartime behavior, adding somewhat apologetically: "You see: I have a bad conscience."[76] A year earlier, in February 1950, Arendt had met with Heidegger in Freiburg.

The Commission on European Jewish Cultural Reconstruction was established under the auspices of prominent American Jewish scholars in the mid-1940s to recover Hebraica and Judaica appropriated by the Germans. The Germans euphemistically called the stolen property "abandoned" (*herrenlos*) to save face before the world. On behalf of the commission, Arendt, who worked first as research director and later as executive director, went to Europe, specifically to Germany, in late 1949 to take stock of the remnants of Jewish cultural treasures. Gershom Scholem performed the same task in Czechoslovakia.

In December Arendt had a long-awaited reunion with Karl and Gertrud Jaspers in Basel, Switzerland. Jaspers "showed me his correspondence with Heidegger," she wrote to her husband. She in turn told Jaspers about her youthful affair with Heidegger. "Ah, how very exciting," Jaspers responded. "[I]nimitable," Arendt commented, obviously impressed by the open-mindedness of the traditional sixty-six-year-old philosopher.[77]

Heidegger, his philosophy, and his life since 1933 had been much on the minds of his two "best friends," so during her visit they spoke frequently though circumspectly about him. Each had reservations, if not hard feelings, especially regarding his support of Nazi ideology, and neither had yet disentangled the emotional upheavals Heidegger had left in their lives. "Whether I'll see Heidegger, I don't know yet," Arendt wrote to Bluecher on 3 January 1950. "I'm leaving it to chance." She continued as though thinking aloud: Heidegger's "letters to Jaspers that he gave me to read sound just like before: the same medley of genuiness and constant lying, or rather cowardice. . . . After my visit with Jaspers I feel less keen to see Heidegger."[78] Two days later she informed Bluecher that she would be in Freiburg—"I must"— presumably on business, but "I don't have the slightest desire to see this gentleman [*den Herrn*]."[79] Yet she got in touch with the Romance scholar Hugo Friedrich, Heidegger's colleague and her fellow student, to obtain Heidegger's address.

On the day of her arrival in Freiburg, 7 February 1950, Arendt wrote Heidegger a note telling him the name of her hotel and suggesting that he come to see her. At 6:30 P.M. Heidegger came to deliver his written answer since there was no telephone in his house and the post-cum-telephone office was already closed.

"That evening and that [the next] morning are a confirmation of a whole life. In fact, a never-expected confirmation," Arendt wrote to Heidegger on 9 February. "When the waiter announced your name (I hadn't really expected you since I hadn't yet received your letter) it was as though suddenly time had stopped. Then, in a flash, I became aware—I have never before admitted it, not to myself and not to you and not to anyone else—that the force of my impulse, after Friedrich gave me your address, has mercifully saved me from committing the only truly unforgivable disloyalty, from mishandling my life. But you must know one thing (since we have not communicated much or very often) that had I done so, it would have been out of pride only—that is, out of pure, plain, crazy stupidity. Not for any reason."[80] The "reason" was, presumably, his Nazi affiliation.

The letter that Arendt had not yet received, since Heidegger had left it at the reception desk before asking the waiter to announce him, was a short, formal greeting, addressing her, as in his first letter to her in 1925, with the formal *sie*. He invited Arendt to come to his house at 8 P.M., where his wife would have gladly welcomed her had she not had a previous engagement. In a cursory remark he informed Arendt that his wife was privy to their past love affair.

So, during "that evening," which Arendt spent alone with Heidegger in his house, the unread letter in her handbag, she was unaware that Heidegger had confessed his infidelity to his wife. Arendt learned about it late at night, when "half-asleep" she read his note in the taxicab on her way back to the hotel. That she was unaware of his confession during the only hours they spent alone together left her free to be open-minded in an atmosphere as yet unclouded by the surprising news—she was convinced, incorrectly, that Elfride Heidegger had "squeezed" the confession out of her husband— just as it left Heidegger free to play on her emotions. He was honest and open as never before, Arendt reported to Bluecher the next day: "For the first time in our lives we really spoke to one another, it seems to me."[81]

Yet it was not until her letter of 9 February, written after a return visit the next morning at Heidegger's request, that she told Heidegger for the first time that she had left Marburg in 1926 because of him. It seems that the old pattern still applied: he talked, she listened. In need of a trusting, understanding friend—this was also meant for Jaspers, whom, Heidegger rightly assumed, Arendt would duly inform—he let her see not the famous philosopher but an aging man broken by vicious slander and accusations of trespasses he had neither committed nor even knew about; he was maligned and vilified merely because (as Arendt would report to Jaspers in 1951) then some "devil" had possessed him. How and why this had happened "he really does not know," Arendt assured Jaspers.[82] She listened to Heidegger, responsive, compassionate, shaken by his ordeal.

Once the relationship was reestablished between the master and his disciple, there was nothing Arendt would not do for him. She confirmed this in the letter of 9 February: "I came [the next morning, 8 February] without knowing what your wife expected of me. . . . Had I known, I wouldn't have hesitated [to come] for a single moment." Evidently Elfride Heidegger made some remarks about German and Jewish women, for Arendt wrote: "I have never felt like a German woman, and have long since ceased to feel like a Jewish woman. I feel like who I really am—a girl from far away" ("Ein Maedchen aus der Fremde," a poem by Friedrich Schiller).[83]

To Bluecher, whom she told only that Heidegger promptly appeared at her hotel upon her arrival in Freiburg (the exact circumstances she described in a letter to her close friend Hilde Frankel), she wrote on 8 February: "This morning an argument with his wife. For the last twenty-five years, or ever since she somehow squeezed the story out of him, she apparently never stopped making life for him hell on earth. And he, who of course lies notoriously always and at each opportunity, had also apparently, as this odd conversation among the three of us proved, never denied, during all the twenty-five years, that [I] was once the passion of his life. I'm afraid his wife is ready to drown all the Jews as long as I am alive. Alas, she is simply stupendously stupid."[84]

On the same day Heidegger wrote a letter to Arendt, who had already left Freiburg. In it he blamed himself alone for abusing his wife's trust, especially because he knew that not only would she have understood the richness of Arendt's and his love but also that she would have blessed the gift bestowed on him by destiny. Now came the time to right the wrong toward the woman to whom he owed everything, who devoted her life to make his productive, comfortable, and fulfilled.

If Arendt still entertained doubts as to the price Heidegger expected her to pay for the privilege of maintaining their relationship, his letters promptly disabused her. He saw the conversation between his wife and his former mistress not as an "argument," as did Arendt, but as a spontaneous reconciliation, one that established a trust among all three of them in an atmosphere of clarity and openness. His wife's loyalty and the confidence she had in her husband and in Hannah, and in Arendt and Heidegger's love, elevated his love for Elfride to new heights. He insisted that Arendt become as close to his wife as he felt that she had already become to Hannah.

In his inimitable fashion Heidegger wrote to Arendt that it was Elfride who helped him and Hannah resume their friendship and that it was Elfride's love that sustained his and Arendt's love. The image of the two women embracing as they parted was how he wanted to see them in the future: emotionally tied by their love for him. Afterward, Elfride was present in almost all his letters, sending Hannah kisses, greetings, regards. The three stood at the threshold of a new experience, one in which Hannah Arendt belonged to both Martin and Elfride Heidegger.

That there was more to Arendt's meeting with Heidegger's wife than she cared to tell Heinrich Bluecher (for the moment, at least) is clear from her 9 February letter to Heidegger and a letter she wrote to his wife.

To Heidegger she wrote: "I was and still am shaken by the honesty and forcefulness of [Elfride's] approach." In the course of the "odd" conversation Arendt had been overcome by a "sudden feeling of solidarity" with Elfride and by a "sudden, overwhelming, deep compassion" for her. But she told Heidegger bluntly: "I could add objectively that I had not of course kept silent out of discretion only but also out of pride. And also out of my love for you—to make nothing more difficult than it already was. I left Marburg exclusively because of you."[85]

The last sentence, an admission it took Arendt twenty-five years to make, casts doubt on her perception that they "really spoke" to one another two days before. Though she did not dare to speak about herself, Heidegger did not hesitate to let her understand that he needed a goodwill ambassador and that Hannah fit the bill. It appears that Arendt accepted the assignment. Most important, she was a renowned Jew, and therefore her support could help neutralize the persistent accusations of Heidegger's antisemitism.

However, Arendt's "Dear Mrs. Heidegger" letter, dated 10 February 1950, suggests that Heidegger's enthusiastic vision of the harmonious and spontaneous closeness of the two women was not realized. Though at times amazingly frank, insofar as it was written to a complete stranger, Arendt's letter is formal, earnest, and businesslike. Arendt was writing out of her own "need" to a woman who she knew resented her because of her husband's infatuation and because Arendt was a Jewess. The letter's authority and poise, its exquisite style and multilayered contents could not but strike the addressee as proof of Arendt's fine mind and spirit, another blow to Elfride Heidegger.

Arendt wrote in answer to Heidegger's letter of 9 February, which she believed his wife had read. Arendt also assumed that Heidegger would read the letter to his wife, so she wrote in fact to both of them. She was letting Elfride Heidegger know that she expected her to act as a censor, not necessarily a compliment, and that she accepted it with grace. "I am happy that I came and I am happy that everything went well," she wrote, another innocuous poke, since they both knew that not everything went well; it was Arendt's bow in Heidegger's direction. "There is a guilt stemming from reserve, which has little to do with lack of trust. In this sense, it seems to me, Martin and I have probably sinned against one another as much as against you," Arendt wrote. "This is not an apology. You expected none," she asserted, perhaps peremptorily, "and I could not give you any.

"You broke the ice," she admitted, "and for this I thank you with all my heart." Clearly Frau Heidegger did have some questions concerning the past, and she expected some explanations. "That is why it did not occur to me that you expected anything from me, because—in connection with this love affair—I committed later so many worse offenses that I didn't get to these earlier events. You see, when I left Marburg, I was absolutely determined never to love a man again, and then I married, just someone, without loving him." Arendt made this admission, which violated her deep sense of privacy, only, it seems, to tell Heidegger once more that she loved him even though she had married Guenther Stern. Perhaps she wanted to evoke in his mind the picture of herself standing alone at the train station as he and Stern left together.

"You have surely never made a secret of your sentiments, nor do you today, including how they relate to me. This sentiment brings matters to such a pass that a conversation is almost impossible, because whatever the other person might say is beforehand characterized and, pardon me, categorized —Jewish, German, Chinese. I am ready at any time, as I indicated to Martin, to discuss these matters in an objective political fashion—I imagine I know something about them —but on condition that the personal-human will be excluded. An ad hominem argument ruins any understanding because it involves something that remains outside man's freedom."

During the conversation—or the argument—Elfride Heidegger suggested inviting Karl Jaspers to act as an arbiter, whether between the women or the Heideggers is not clear. "How did you come up with the idea to invite Jaspers to act as an arbiter?" Arendt asked. "Only because you happen to know that we are friends? Or perhaps you have so much confidence in him?" she inquired sarcastically, aware that Elfride barely knew Jaspers and had not seen him since the early 1930s. "I was so taken aback that I didn't react; now I can't get rid of the question," which, she added graciously, Mrs. Heidegger should feel free not to answer. "We will meet again soon," she ended. "Until then please accept this as greetings and thanks."[86]

The meeting opened a chapter in the relationship between Arendt and Heidegger that was to last twenty-five years. It was punctuated by periods of lively correspondence and by protracted silences, by visits carefully arranged and usually supervised by Elfride Heidegger, and rare hours, which Arendt treasured, spent with Heidegger alone. The silences imposed by Heidegger (resembling those of the late 1920s and 1930s) ensued from his fluctuating moods, whims, his drive to control, and once only from Arendt's independent stand, which he perceived as defiance and swiftly punished by silence.

Arendt's and Heidegger's differing versions of the 1950

meeting reflect their different perceptions, not deliberate distortions. Heidegger wanted to see solidarity between his wife and Hannah, but Arendt knew that there was an un-bridgeable division between herself and Elfride Heidegger. Arendt realized that she did not know the Heidegger with whom she fell in love twenty-five years before. She learned to accept him, however, often rebelling internally and be-lieving, incorrectly, that now she knew him inside out, as she indicated in her letters to Heinrich Bluecher. Moreover, she was convinced that she alone could understand the depth of his soul, that she possessed the strength to pour life into him, that she was his muse and his healer. Because of their spiritual tie, he needed her more than he did anyone else, as she frequently wrote to her husband. In fact, she needed him to need her.

In mid-February, seven days after her departure, Heideg-ger wrote to invite her to return at the beginning of March. And on 2 March 1950, Arendt paid him another visit. His offer to make the hotel arrangements indicated his prefer-ence for a longer rather than a shorter stay. This time she came for four days. Obviously Mrs. Heidegger agreed to the invitation, for when she objected in later years, Heidegger followed her wish.

It seems that Arendt's second visit was more fulfilling for both of them, in a private sense, than the first one. The drama of the first encounter, after what Heidegger called a quarter of a century, and the inevitable tension affected the atmosphere no more. For the first and last time Arendt told

Heidegger how much she had suffered because of him. Recalling that visit in a letter dated 4 May 1950, Heidegger for once openly wrote about the pain he had caused her and about his own failings, which, he said, he no longer concealed from himself. Calling her "*Vertrauteste*" (most trusted friend), he spoke rather melodramatically about the light that came into their lives and about the communion of their hearts.

Evidently they had also discussed Heidegger's behavior toward Jaspers, for on 7 March Arendt explained to Bluecher: "The only reason Heidegger suddenly stopped seeing Jaspers [in 1933] was that he had realized what he had actually done and he was ashamed. He was completely taken aback that Jaspers could have interpreted it in another way, namely as a boycott of his Jewish wife. In fact, he associated a great deal in these years with other people who were in a similar situation; the most obvious explanation had never occurred to him."[87] There is no evidence, however, that Heidegger associated with any Germans who, like Jaspers, had Jewish wives. Nor did Heidegger mention even one such name to Arendt, because they or their spouses generally went into exile.

After the 1950 visits Arendt—who had only one year earlier vehemently opposed the publication of Heidegger's work—became his devoted if unpaid agent in the United States, finding publishers, negotiating contracts, and selecting the best translators. Above all, she did what she could to whitewash his Nazi past. Even Elfride Heidegger came to respect Arendt's connections in America and her usefulness. For Heidegger it was natural to regard her labors as a privilege he accorded her, for in so doing he proved that he trusted her.

Heinrich Bluecher, a great admirer of Heidegger's philosophy, was no doubt impressed by the role his wife played in Heidegger's life and work, and he saw her efforts as a contribution to philosophy rather than as a continuation of an emotional involvement. It would be wrong to assume that either Arendt or Bluecher perceived Heidegger as a threat to their marriage, as Elfride Heidegger perceived Arendt with regard to hers. Bluecher—realistic, straightforward, a stranger to the ambiguous temptations that accompanied Arendt's first experience of love—wrote off the youthful romance as something that belonged to the sphere of fond memories. He encouraged Arendt to be at Heidegger's side for the sake of philosophy. Arendt could not have continued her friendship with Heidegger had she not had Bluecher's love and support. The feelings she had for Heidegger went beyond sexual and psychological definitions. Bluecher, however, was her other self. She could live without Heidegger, but she could not live without Bluecher. She mistrusted Heidegger as much as she trusted Bluecher, and for her, trust was the foundation of a genuine union. Regardless of the perceived irrationality of her emotions for Heidegger, she could not love a man she did not respect. She exculpated him not as much out of loyalty, compassion, or a sense of justice as out of her own need to save her pride and dignity.

The letters Heidegger wrote following Arendt's visits were warm, elegant, romantic, even seductive. He would recall her becoming dress, ask for her photographs, compose poems for her, remember a symphony by Beethoven they both enjoyed, describe the magic of nature, hark back to the long-ago past. Then, in odd contrast, he would describe to her the beautiful flowers he saw from his study—flowers, he told her, tended by his wife.

The sixteen letters Heidegger wrote Arendt in 1950 stand out from the other postwar ones both in quantity and substance. They were followed by six in 1951, three in 1952, two in 1953, and one in 1959; in his old age he needed again to talk with her, and their correspondence revived.

Several of Heidegger's 1950 letters resemble the letters he had written her when their love affair flourished. His practical considerations aside, Heidegger was touched and flattered by the durability of Arendt's feelings for him, which had withstood his alliance with the Nazis. He told her that the catastrophe which was to befall Germany was already clear to him in 1937 and 1938. But was it? His activities and his behavior—in April 1938 he did not attend Husserl's funeral—until the end of the war tell a different story.

The reappearance of Arendt in his life forced Heidegger to mollify both his wife and Arendt. So in one letter he would write that he needed his wife's love and Hannah's love, too; that his and Hannah's love needed Elfride's love, for love breeds love. In another letter he would say that he looked long into Arendt's face (in a picture) and that the pain in her eyes reflected the rough treatment the world gave her and the experiences of a mature woman. The mystery of the transformation is embodied in a Greek goddess, he wrote: a woman is concealed in a girl, a girl in a woman. And he wondered what was more beautiful: Hannah's letter or her picture.

In early May, Heidegger went to Messkirch for three weeks. Between 3 May and 16 May he sent four letters to Arendt in quick succession. Clearly he could not write that often from home or express himself so unrestrainedly. Even though he missed Hannah, he wrote, every day since she had come back brought him joy. In prose studded with flourishes he wrote that Hannah alone was close to him when he was thinking; that he dreamed about her living nearby and of running his fingers through her hair; that her heart dwelled in his heart, and so did hope and longing. Heidegger sounded in his Messkirch letters like a changed man, excited and effervescent. Not once did he mention his wife. It was as though only he and Hannah existed.

After he returned to Freiburg the everyday worries set in: the miserable pension, his sick daughter-in-law, the mistreatment he suffered from the government and church authorities, his fear of the Russians and their secret agents, who, he swore, would never get him alive. The peace of mind he had in Messkirch vanished; his letters were often disjointed and plaintive, but the spark rekindled by Arendt's presence reappeared now and then.

Yet the correspondence from May left a mark, however

briefly. Heidegger asked Arendt not to be troubled should an "eruption" break out at his home during her planned visit in February 1951 (she did not go). And he asked her to answer his Messkirch letters with caution. The secrecy and mystery brought back their past love affair.

At Heidegger's request Arendt sent him a picture of her mother, whom Heidegger had met in the early 1920s. He wanted somehow to "catch up" on the years when they were separated, but they both knew that it was an illusion. Arendt's letters were censored, her visits unwelcome, her presents—records, books, a set of Kafka's works, a silk scarf for Elfride—suspect.

The letters Heidegger wrote Arendt in 1950 reflect his short-lived desire to retrieve the glory of love and power.

Ten

In March 1952, Hannah Arendt went to Europe again on behalf of the Commission on Jewish Cultural Reconstruction. She also planned to explore the totalitarian elements of Marxism for a book on Marx. She shifted her focus to the Marxist elements of Soviet totalitarianism after critics pointed out her failure to substantiate her claim in *The Origins of Totalitarianism* that Nazism and Bolshevism were comparable ideologies. Published in 1951, the book brought Arendt a worldwide fame that she knew Heidegger would find hard to swallow. Princeton University invited her to become the first woman to give the prestigious Christian Gaus Seminars—the emphasis on "first woman" annoyed her—another irritant for Heidegger. Bluecher wrote her facetiously: "Heidegger will have a new reason to regret that he introduced a woman to philosophy." "Yes, Jaspers will be pleased," Arendt answered, "and Heidegger—I will see him tomorrow—will be less pleased, but I couldn't care less."[88]

As though to distance herself from Heidegger she substituted "Freiburg" for his name in her next letters to Bluecher. "I have finally written to Freiburg; first I let him stew, withholding my address. Now I fixed [my visit] for May 19, and I will take it from there." For once she had the upper hand, and the satisfaction she took in this tiny victory indicates what a rare feat it was. "Relieved, he wrote that now he knows at least where I am. Difficulties with Madame are quite obvious. Perhaps she is also furious that Jaspers treated her husband *en canaille,* and she probably lays the blame at my door. In short—a mess."[89] What was obvious to Arendt did not necessarily correspond with the facts revealed during her visit. She planned to stay in Freiburg for a week, and, concerned that the visit might become public knowledge, she camouflaged it as a business trip. Why there was a need for conspiracy is unclear, unless she wanted to relive the enforced secrecy of their trysts in the past.

Though Arendt expected no warm welcome from Elfride Heidegger, scarves and greetings notwithstanding, she was taken aback by her behavior. "The woman is jealous almost to the point of madness," she reported to Bluecher in May from Freiburg. "After the years of apparently nursing the hope that he would simply forget me, her jealousy only intensified. In his absence she made a half-antisemitic scene with me. Anyway the political persuasion of the lady (I'll bring or send you, when I have a chance, her favorite newspaper, the most repulsive smearsheet I have yet seen in Germany), her narrow-mindedness, her stupidity untouched by all experiences, reeking with ugly resentment, makes everything directed against him easily understandable. . . . To cut a long story short I made him a regular scene, and afterwards the situation improved considerably." That it was Heidegger himself who deserved "everything directed against him" did not cross Arendt's mind. What he did, said, and wrote over a period of twelve years—in particular, during his rectorship—seemed immaterial to her. In her zeal to blame everything on Elfride Heidegger, Arendt sided with those who presented her as a sinister force.

"Perhaps all this is meaningless since he is in splendid shape," Arendt continues. "He read to me long parts of his lectures, for which he prepares himself in a truly touching manner (he always writes a lecture twice, and many pages four or five times)."

Arendt more than once entertained the idea of meeting with Heidegger away from his wife, away from his home. She firmly believed that she could best help him if the two of them were alone. Now, too, she made tentative plans: "I'm not sure whether I won't meet with Martin once more, somewhere," in August, she wrote to Bluecher. She would have then to postpone coming back, and her husband would have to go for vacation alone, which she knew was "absolutely dreadful" for him. "But what should I do?" she asked rhetorically.

"Had I not grown a little wiser, Stups [Arendt's nickname for her husband], I couldn't have gone through with it. I feel I can manage, but I also feel that, God knows, it isn't going to be easy. There is on the other hand [my] certitude of a fundamentally good nature—absolutely convincing to me, but, in fact, inconceivable to anyone else—of a trust that never ceases to affect me deeply (I can hardly describe it differently); and there is a complete absence—as soon as we are alone together—of all these things that otherwise emerge so easily; and there is his genuine helplessness and defenselessness. As long as he can work there is no danger;

the only thing I'm afraid of are his recurring periods of depression. I am trying to fortify him against the depression. Perhaps he will remember when I'm no longer here."[90]

Bluecher was sympathetic to his wife's plight. "It would be irresponsible," he answered, "in view of Martin's situation, not to do everything possible to pour some strength into him. So, stay there as long as you can, as long as it makes sense. Forget the wife: when stupidity turns into stubbornness, ultimately it grows into evil, or in any case cannot be distinguished from evil. Keep silent and ignore it. What is called thinking? [the title of Heidegger's work published in 1954] is one of the most wonderful philosophical questions after God. So help him to ask it."[91] He kept reassuring Hannah: "You have certainly done all the right things, but it is a dismal situation, such a messed-up life. And all this because of dumb prejudice and weakness of the social backbone. Such society deserves nothing but to go to hell, and it seems it will. If at least his manuscripts could be saved."[92]

Naturally Bluecher was familiar only with Arendt's version of the situation: the obnoxious behavior of Elfride Heidegger toward Hannah and her detrimental influence, to say the least, on Heidegger's private and public life. He remained unfamiliar with Heidegger's inner conviction, frequently expressed in his letters to Arendt, regarding his wife's loyalty and care, his love for and reliance on her, and his attachment to the life they had shared over three decades. On the strength of Arendt's words Bluecher came to know the private Heidegger as she described him, or rather as he existed in her imagination: a man who married the wrong woman and thus ruined his life, and who, had he not been bogged down by obsolete social mores, would have left her, saved the remnants of his wretched life, and let himself be protected and inspired by Hannah. Arendt was courted and loved by many men, but she was not in the habit of bragging about it; on the contrary, she seldom mentioned it, and then only to close friends, playing it down in a gentle, jocular fashion. But Heidegger was different from other men. What truly mattered to her was not erotic attraction, which may or may not have existed—she was sensual without being strongly sexual—but the special role that she believed she played in his life, the spiritual kinship that she believed he shared with no one else. Arendt convinced herself, regardless of what Heidegger repeatedly told her, that Elfride was the source of all her husband's misfortunes, that she undermined his prestige and created an atmosphere of hostility around him. Had Arendt's first husband, Guenther Stern, not told her about it, Arendt may well have been ignorant of Elfride Heidegger's early allegiance to National Socialism, and she could hardly have known that the ideology was shared and that it brought the couple even closer together. She did not, after all, believe that it was Heidegger's ideology. Just as she exonerated Heidegger from his Nazi past, she attributed Mrs. Heidegger's current "political persuasion" to a right-wing smearsheet creed, thus setting them apart when they belonged together. For how could Heidegger, endowed with a "fundamentally good nature," have reconciled himself to his wife's reactionary views? Arendt imagined him help-less and defenseless, suffering at the hands of this evil woman. Only if one recognized her resentments, biases, and stupidity could one understand her pernicious influence. By shifting the entire blame for Heidegger's past onto his wife, Arendt absolved him, the personification of the *Geist,* of any responsibility and therefore could in good conscience re-sume the role of muse and, most significantly, come to terms with herself and her fascination with him.

Regardless of Mrs. Heidegger's behavior, Arendt intended, after the one-week visit in May, to see Heidegger once more before leaving Europe. "I'll probably meet with Martin, in greatest secrecy, somwhere near the Bodensee," she wrote to Bluecher on 24 May 1952. On 30 May she informed him from Basel, where she was visiting Jaspers, that after some more travel in Germany, she would go to London and Paris: "[W]hat next, I still don't know. It depends also on Freiburg." The letter unfinished, she drove to the Basel train station where, before boarding the train, she added, "in haste": "I am going to Freiburg."[93]

Heidegger's note dated 5 June 1952, requesting Arendt to abstain both from writing and from coming, either did not reach her in time or else spurred her to go. On 6 June she wrote Bluecher from Stuttgart:

Freiburg ended with new scenes made by the lady. I really don't know what to do. The lecture [Heidegger's] was again magnificent, although he was in bad shape and read poorly. . . . His son, with whom I attended the lecture, remarked afterwards: [Y]es, here blows a completely abstract wind. . . . Martin spoke [to me] with frightening objectivity. Obviously he dreads the moment when both his sons will leave the house [Heidegger's sons were aged thirty-one and thirty] and his wife will lose the only thing that gives meaning to her life. He was always in the second place, therefore he had peace. This, however, will change now because before long the sons will leave. The whole story is really a tragedy. While she does not know what to do with herself and is being simply mean, over there, in Messkirch, there are 50,000 untyped pages she could have comfortably typed over all these years. And of course now it is too late to save them. In reality he has one friend only—his brother.*

Most illuminating is the lady's library, which I have carefully examined. Among approximately 100 books a complete collection of Gertrud Baeumer and a pile of trash.‡ Among them there are a dozen decent books, all gifts from him, with his inscription. But it didn't help much. When I imagine that he will be forced to return to this milieu when he no longer can work, I get simply dizzy.[94]

*Heidegger's brother, Fritz, typed all his manuscripts; Elfride Heidegger never did. Courtesy Hugo Ott.

‡Gertrud Baeumer was a leading figure in the German women's movement, editor of a Nazi-oriented women's magazine, and author of popular novels.

Arendt, by now in London, could not stop thinking about "Freiburg." Her visit cut short—presumably by Martin Heidegger himself, since he had requested that she cancel the visit—and her goal to "stabilize" Heidegger unachieved, she felt wretched. Heidegger's admission of concern for his sons—it impressed Arendt no end that he confided in her— was proof in Arendt's eyes of his estrangement from his family. In fact, it was probably proof that he had never before broached a personal subject with her. Yet seventeen years earlier he had shared similar concerns with Elisabeth Blochmann, so Arendt's notion of his objectivity was entirely subjective. As were her conclusions.

Arendt claimed that it was Elfride Heidegger who made all the decisions on behalf of her husband, including those concerning his relations with colleagues and students, and that because of her there was nothing but hostility between him and "literally everybody." Perhaps so. By isolating him, creating a situation in which he had but one friend—his wife—she could control him as never before. Still, it does not seem plausible that Heidegger, a strong-willed, determined man, could be so manipulated by her. Perhaps, exhausted by the five years of de-nazification, all he wanted was peace in which to work, and for this he was ready to trade his friends, including Arendt. Elfride Heidegger, at fifty-nine, was understandably bitter: the Nazi dream dashed, her people outcasts in the world, her once-powerful husband fending off constant attacks, her children gone, and a stubborn Jewess looming on the horizon. Her husband, at sixty-three, always an avid sportsman, was in excellent shape, creative, popular, surrounded by disciples and acolytes, male and female. He was as attractive to women and attracted by women as he had been since she met him.

It was not beyond him to play a game in front of Arendt, to stir her emotions, evoke her compassions, and use her. Heidegger "does not know how to conduct himself," Arendt despaired. "He is spinning in a whirl, spotting this or that aspect of a matter at one time or another. At the moment he is sick, more or less, from exasperation, and I don't plan to go again to Freiburg," she informed Bluecher, passing over Heidegger's request that she not come. "There is absolutely nothing I can do. Whether I managed to stabilize him just a bit for the years to come, I don't know. I tried. He needs peace in any case, and that she [Elfride] doesn't let him have, certainly not when I am around. . . . This does not mean that anything has changed between us; this really seems no longer possible."[95] But she was wrong.

"The story with Heidegger is dreadful, quite dreadful," Bluecher replied. "But don't worry, now, his creativity will never fade away. . . . So, in spite of everything, he will go on. He just needs a young girl to work on his manuscripts, and a young girl or a youngish lady will eventually turn up," he wrote, only half in jest, probably believing, and rightly so, that such company would not be unwelcome to the philosopher.[96]

Arendt was not amused. She appreciated neither Bluecher's tone nor his jocular suggestion. A young girl was the last remedy she would wish for Heidegger. There was no place in the life of the spirit for matters of the flesh, she was convinced. "Young" sounded like an outright insult. Irritably, she retorted: "In fact, for the time being at least there is nothing 'dreadful' with Martin, only sad. Nothing changed and nothing is going to change." She might have been repeating, to reassure herself, that nothing would change between herself and Heidegger, already sensing that her prediction was not certain.

"[']I'm always so frightened,['] Martin, quite disheartened, said to me before the lecture, the manuscript ready in his hand." This image of Heidegger was further proof of his unrestrained frankness, another confirmation of his enduring trust in Arendt, which she knew her husband would appreciate. And she wanted to reassure Bluecher—who was in a panic, preparing two new courses for the New School—that even experienced teachers suffered from stage fright.

Heidegger's tarnished reputation troubled her constantly. "When Alfred [Kazin] told me quite naïvely that the name Heidegger seems to have become a sort of a 'cuss word' in Germany, in academic and even other circles, I was quite distressed," she wrote to Bluecher from Munich on 20 June. "I cannot change anything. Out of sheer desperation and an inability to write a single letter himself, he lets his wife take care of everything and puts his signature on every piece of paper."[97] That Heidegger did this because he trusted his wife's judgment or because it was convenient for him to relegate some matters to her did not seem to occur to

Arendt. Her contempt for Elfride Heidegger was limitless, and, moreover, the wife's position of privilege may well have grated on her nerves.

It might also have been that Heidegger wished simply to evoke Arendt's compassion, to shed all responsibility, as was his custom, or to pit one woman against the other while keeping both on his side. In 1952, after Arendt published *The Origins of Totalitarianism,* her fame was growing, and Heidegger, much as he resented her prominence, recognized her growing usefulness and now and then threw her a crumb.

Bluecher did not always take at face value Arendt's assumption that Elfride Heidegger alone was at fault for antagonizing the people who approached her husband. Professor Karl Loewith, with whom the Heideggers met in Rome in 1936, paid a visit to his former teacher "in good faith, and then some words fell which again spoiled everything," Arendt informed Bluecher, adding: "It is of course always Frau Heidegger who has the last word" and manages to inject animosity, as was the case with Loewith. Loewith criticized Heidegger's concept of history, and this, not Elfride Heidegger's interference, most certainly led to the falling out. "Heidegger was terribly hurt" by Loewith's apostasy, Arendt wrote.[98] "Don't misunderstand me, I surely agree with you about Loewith," Bluecher answered. "If one cannot outdistance one's master but remains a pupil, one should not pass oneself off for the interpreter of the master. And one should not pelt the master with his own stones. But this master cut off this normal track for his students, especially the Jewish students, and thus everything is poisoned."[99]

From Germany Arendt traveled to England. Heidegger's situation continued to worry her, but she did gain some perspective. "In no way is it his wife only, but also his sons, and he himself" who were to blame for Heidegger's problems, she wrote Bluecher from Manchester in late June. Her admission that Heidegger too was responsible for his problems was a serious departure from her former opinion that "everything" that went wrong in his life was exclusively his wife's fault. "[T]his time he spoke very often [with me] and almost complained (something he had never done before); he sees [the situation] for what it really is, but evidently only when I am right there in the middle—like a pickerel in a carp pond."[100] She assumed that her presence somehow crystallized for Heidegger his family problems, but what precisely she meant is not clear.

England, "the most *civilized* country on earth [written in English] but also the most boring," soothed her after the nerve-wracking visit in Freiburg. "Cambridge is a dream," she wrote Bluecher, "and very, very peculiar, as everything in England. One can have a very interesting and sensible conversation here. I have fun."[101] She lectured, went sightseeing and shopping—spending loads of money on exquisite sweaters and pullovers for herself and Heinrich and growing anxious slightly over it—but what she really wanted was to be back with her husband. "Soon I will be with you again, where I belong."[102]

And with Bluecher was where she belonged, no matter how preoccupied she might have been with Heidegger—"the Martin legend," Bluecher called him—no matter how involved with him and his affairs.[103] Her entanglement with Heidegger's problems, personal and professional, the watchful eye of Elfride Heidegger, and the atmosphere of impending doom exasperated and exhausted her. Bluecher was her only haven, and the longer she was away from him and the deeper she was torn by Heidegger's trials, the more she missed the security her husband gave her. Heidegger made her miserable, Bluecher wrote from sweltering New York (she implored him to buy an air conditioner, a recurrent topic in many letters; he thought the cost too high), but he knew she could still enjoy herself, not because of her inexhaustible strength but because of her spirited, vivacious nature.

Back in Germany in mid-July, Arendt lectured on "Terror and Ideology" at the University of Marburg where she had met Heidegger almost three decades before, and at the University of Heidelberg, where she was Jaspers's doctoral student. "Marburg is completely dead intellectually," she wrote to Bluecher. In particular she deplored the fate of Heidegger's legacy and worried—"that is, worried for him," she explained—"about the trendiness of his fame."[104] Heidelberg's "pseudo-intellectualism" was only a little better. The level of instruction was shamefully low, "feeble-minded" professors agreed that " 'metaphysics is entirely superfluous,' " and the general atmosphere was sectarian, cliquish. "It is a terrible witch's cauldron, and I am happy it is none of my concern."[105]

No sooner did Arendt return to New York than she set out to repair Heidegger's tainted image, just as he expected her to do. On 23 August 1952 she wrote a letter to the Reverend John M. Oesterreicher, a Catholic priest of Jewish extraction, "to correct my own statement on Heidegger." Ironically, Arendt retracted but Heidegger did not. "This statement and a number of similar attacks were based on rumors which through a consistent persistency over many years appeared like reliable information," she wrote. She explained, as Jaspers did to her in 1948, that the "circular letter" which Heidegger signed as rector was addressed to "all Jewish teachers of the University . . . not . . . to Husserl personally." Also, she admitted that "sometime during the war" (in 1941) Heidegger agreed to have the dedication to Husserl eliminated from the reissued *Being and Time,* "but that was already a time of open terror, and I think he can prove that he did so only under strong pressure.* But even then he did not yield to the point of suppressing the footnotes in which Husserl's work is mentioned," she clarified. She wanted Oesterreicher to see the facts in their proper context: "The relationship between Husserl and Heidegger had very much deteriorated prior to 1933, so that one can hardly say that

*"Dedicated to Edmund Husserl in respect and friendship. Todtnauberg, Black Forest, 8 April 1926."

Heidegger broke with Husserl as a result of the events of 1933."[106]

All that was true. More or less. Heidegger failed Husserl in purely human terms only. It was not a matter of disagreeing with Husserl on philosophical grounds, which had happened before 1933, but of breaking contact at a time when Husserl was being persecuted as a Jew, of ostentatiously failing to attend his funeral, and of not offering condolences to Malvina Husserl. (Elfride Heidegger wrote a letter of condolence for both of them.) He might have indeed removed his dedication to Husserl "under strong pressure" from his publisher, but not, it should be noted, from a more dangerous agency; he might also have desisted from reissuing the book without falling victim to the "open terror."

Heidegger often mentioned Husserl to Arendt in his letters in the 1920s, invariably with reverence and gratitude. She knew at the time, as did Jaspers, that he was a frequent guest in the Husserls' home, that the two philosophers were tied by more than their professional relationship, and that it was Husserl who submitted Heidegger's name as his successor to the faculty and was instrumental in securing the appointment. The conflicting emotions Heidegger stirred in Arendt and in Jaspers because of his behavior toward Husserl are evident in the metamorphosis Arendt's opinion underwent from 1946, when she called Heidegger a potential murderer of Husserl, to her 1952 letter to the Reverend Oesterreicher; and in Jaspers's withholding from

Arendt for twenty years facts about Heidegger, the man in power.

Karl Jaspers had been an authority for Arendt ever since she became his student: "[W]hen I was young you were the only person who brought me up."[107] As an adult she looked up to him as a teacher but also as a trusted, wise friend. He was one of the few people whose opinion carried enormous weight for her. Had he not been at odds with himself about Heidegger, Jaspers might have told Arendt what appeared in print only after her death: that Heidegger was a treacherous friend.* But he chose silence, believing perhaps that Heidegger deserved one friend at least—Hannah Arendt. And this role she fulfilled by writing the letter exonerating Heidegger.

Heidegger rightly observed that Arendt was the "and" between "Jaspers and Heidegger."

*In his notes on Heidegger, Jaspers wrote: "He was the only one among my friends with whom I disagreed in 1933, the only one who betrayed me." Hans Saner, ed., *Karl Jaspers Notizen zu Martin Heidegger,* 92. In his autobiography, Jaspers wrote: "He seemed to me like a friend ready to betray one in one's absence." Jaspers, *Philosophische Autobiographie,* 97.

Eleven

The stormy year 1952 ended with a brief note from Heidegger written in December; in it he thanked Arendt for her pictures. During the time of their love affair he had often asked her for a picture. Was he now telling her that the passage of time had not changed them much? But it had. In 1953 she received one letter from him and wrote no letters to him.* Years would go by with no personal communication between them save for occasional birthday or New Year's wishes. Only business—translations and publications of his works in the United States—elicited a more lively correspondence. But then Heidegger would pointedly write about his wife, the vacations they enjoyed together, her physical condition, her efforts to make his life comfortable. He lamented the state of Europe: in fact, Europe no longer existed, he thought. It was moribund because the forces of evil, nihilism, and technology, against which he had fought, ultimately prevailed. Germany and National Socialism, the one country and the single ideology capable of reversing Europe's decline, had failed.

Arendt was doing a good job overseeing the translations, and she was rewarded by Heidegger's praise, sometimes effusive, of her gift for languages, her ability to think and

*Arendt carefully preserved Heidegger's letters. In the 1920s and 1930s she kept only some copies of her letters to him. In the postwar period she kept copies of most of her letters to him.

understand, skills appropriate for a student of his. In a few perfunctory words he would ask about her work before switching to an exhaustive description of his own. Even Elfride Heidegger was pleased about Arendt's devotion to her husband's work, and Arendt was granted the status of a family friend of sorts. A bookstore in Germany mailed her six works by Heidegger, one in a French translation. Arendt promptly answered his "good letter," which was devoted to himself and his work, save for one sentence asking about hers. "You could have hardly given me a greater pleasure," she wrote, obviously delighted that he had broken a long silence. Certainly aware that he asked about her work out of politeness, not genuine interest, she nevertheless dutifully answered that she had been working for the last three years on three topics: the relation between action and speech as distinguished from work and labor, which "I could not [do] . . . had I not learned from you in my youth"; on philosophy and politics, "in your interpretation"; and on the question of authority.[108] His letter at least gave her a chance to pay him a compliment (and she knew how hungry he was for just that) and to allude to the past.

In the fall of 1955, during her European tour, Arendt as usual visited Germany. Earlier that year she had suspected that Heidegger was distancing himself from her. "From Heidegger not a single word," she wrote Bluecher from Berkeley, where she was invited to teach political theory in the spring semester, "although a few months ago I dropped him a few lines. I have no idea what is going on. I have not written him that I am coming to Europe, because at that time it was not definite. What has offended him, or what kind of new suspicions he has conjured up, I don't know. I can't help it [last sentence in English]. Or perhaps he is just busy working."[109] It dawned on her later that what had offended Heidegger was the forthcoming German translation of her *Origins of Totalitarianism,* which, given the wide advance publicity her reputation now warranted, he could not but notice.

Once in Germany, Arendt was again torn by doubts. "Heidegger—I don't know yet what I'll do, but I don't think I'll go to see him," she wrote her husband on 14 November. "The fact that my book must be out just now . . . creates the worst possible constellation. He doesn't know that I'm in the country, but I have in any case the impression that he is not particularly interested in seeing me right now. Reason: see above. . . . I have a feeling that for a while I should let the grass grow a little. . . . As you know I am quite ready to behave toward Heidegger as though I have never written a word and will never write one. And this is the unspoken *conditio sine qua non* of the whole affair. . . . I could do it [see Heidegger] only with enormous difficulty, and I am in no mood for it." Arendt was polishing a lecture she was to deliver in Germany and desperately wanted for once to put her own work above Heidegger. And she was looking for a way to protect herself as she had when she left Marburg, took a lover, and married Guenther Stern. Now she summoned to her defense work and professional obligations. But it did not quite work. "The long and short of it: I am at the brink of doing the same thing I did 30 years ago, and somehow I cannot change it. Caption: following the law that started 'it' off."[110]

This admission puts in a nutshell the long story of Arendt's involvement with Heidegger. Arendt was now forty-six years old, and Heidegger was no longer the enigma he had been to his eighteen-year-old student. Yet she could not resist his spell. Her helplessness dismayed and disquieted her, for it contradicted her healthy instincts. With effort she could play the role of Heidegger's starry-eyed student, but she rebelled because her dignity was at stake. She was asking her husband for help.

"I don't think your feelings about the Heidegger affair are quite right," he responded. "To leave the country without letting him know you were there seems to me very harsh, and I don't quite understand it."[111] Indeed, he did not understand the depth of her dilemma, her fear of being again humiliated and manipulated now by both Martin and Elfride Heidegger, of finding herself in the subordinate position she was in thirty years ago. It was a despair that Bluecher, for all his sensitivity, could not grasp, so alien to him was the self-inflicted romantic suffering. Heidegger was a prominent philosopher (though discredited by his Nazism); therefore he asked the New School of Social Research to extend an invitation to him. Attributing to Heidegger the same need he himself had of Arendt, that of an intellectual partner, he mistook her agony for a failure to act.

Arendt vacillated between what reason told her and what she knew. She did want to liberate herself from Heidegger's power, to put an end to the bondage but not to the bond; she wanted to retain his friendship, and perhaps his love. As a child, she made an extraordinary effort to earn her mother's love by pretending that her feelings for her father were unaffected by his looks, which were disfigured by syphilis; now she was ready to pretend she was not a scholar to retain Heidegger's affection. Insecurity and a need to be loved, which had once led her to bargain away her independence, were as real for the fifty-year-old woman as they were for the five-year-old child. To maintain the role of his confidante she was ready to disavow her mind and accomplishments. But she knew that would not be sufficient for Heidegger. He wanted her to be dependent on him, as she had been in the past. Torn by conflicting sensations, she was at a loss. "Somehow I cannot change it."

Hurt by Bluecher's reproach and misinterpretation, she gave in and revealed some of the most recent facts. "Concerning Heidegger, my dearest, it is not as simple as I briefly described. That I don't go [to see Heidegger] seems to me like a silent agreement between Heidegger and me," she wrote. But now she expressed some of her bitterness:

Ever since I went to Berkeley I haven't actually heard from him. As I've done every year I sent him birthday wishes, from Greece, and gave him my address. He didn't even write on my birthday. Tu vois . . . [Arendt's ellipsis]

He could, couldn't he, figure out counting on his five fingers that I will come to Germany. The reason seems clear to me: on the one hand my book and the professorship (naturally widely publicized in Germany), on the other the situation in Freiburg. He knows what I think about it even without my coming there. This semester he holds one-hour lectures and probably imagines that my visit would be but an unbearable disturbance. And it is likely that it would be just that. When he is lecturing a meeting outside of Freiburg is out of the question. And this would be the only possibility. I could handle all that and just be there, simply go and that's that. But right now I cannot do it because my own work is very much on my mind and he will notice it in 5 minutes.

It was not as much preoccupation with her work as a reasonable suspicion that Heidegger would instantly detect the lack of her full attention that caused her to hold back. Arendt concluded by asking her husband, "But tell me what you think."[112]

This time Bluecher understood. He could deal with facts, not with deeply concealed fears that went back to her youth. "If Heidegger didn't answer you at all, then your assessment of the situation is no doubt correct and there is nothing one can do. What an angst and what an obtuseness."[113]

Heidegger knew of course that Arendt was in Germany, as did everyone who read the newspapers, and simply did not want to meet with her. Her book was prominently displayed in bookstores, especially in university towns. Her lectures drew crowds all over the country, and the interviews she granted were well covered by the press. Hannah Arendt had become a sensation in Germany, not the prodigal daughter but the proud Jewess (she made a point of emphasizing at lectures, interviews, and public appearances that she was a Jew), challenging her own people, who had banished her from her own country.

It seems, however, that Heidegger's motive for avoiding Arendt might have had a much deeper and more fundamental rationale. The main concept of *The Origins of Totalitarianism* most certainly was highly offensive to him. To make things worse, it was the work of his own student and of a woman who, he appeared to think, was still intellectually dependent on him. In her book Arendt equated National Socialism, which he admired, with communism, which he hated. Still worse, she undermined Heidegger's main line of defense: by equating National Socialism with communism Arendt called into question Heidegger's intention to "rescue the Western civilization from the dangers of communism."[114]

It must now have been apparent to Arendt that Heidegger did not need her as badly as she believed to "stabilize" him, to confide in, to inspire him. There is no evidence that he ever acquiesced to meeting her anywhere but in his house. The firm conviction she expressed in 1952, that nothing "has changed between us" and that any change "seems really no longer possible," did not stand the test of time.

Heidegger's old friend Elisabeth Blochmann seems to

have been temperamentally more suited to him than was Arendt. While Arendt, visiting Germany, did not miss a chance to emphasize her Jewishness, though she never did so anywhere else, the half Jewish Blochmann always identified completely with the Germans. In 1933, holding the position of professor of pedagogy at the Pedagogic Academy in Halle / Saale, she pleaded with Heidegger, who was already a rector, to use his connections to help her stay in Germany and participate in "German work in whatever fashion."[115] At the same time, Arendt plagued him with questions about his attitude toward Jews. When Heidegger was not forthcoming, Blochmann went into exile in England; in 1952 she returned to Germany and became a professor of pedagogy at the University of Marburg. She and Heidegger resumed their correspondence. He sent her gifts of his books, she sent him her pictures. "Elfride brought me your dear letter," he wrote to her on 2 November 1955, just when Arendt was anxiously waiting for a word from him. "You gave me a very special pleasure with both your pictures."[116] A year earlier he shared with Blochmann his thoughts on Karl Loewith. "Loewith has no idea about Greek philosophy," Heidegger wrote about his former student. "About *Thinking* he has no idea [either]; perhaps he hates it. I have never met a person who lives so exclusively on resentment and 'anti-.'" Heidegger went on to say that in Marburg Loewith had been the "reddest Marxist" and had considered *Being and Time* at one time "theology in disguise" and at another "pure atheism." Loewith, Heidegger let her know, was guilty of things that

Heidegger didn't even want to bring up, "although I helped him with recommendations in Italy and Japan [in the 1930s]."[117]

In Elisabeth Blochmann, Heidegger had an uncritical listener who could not and would not engage in argument, as Arendt might. Indeed, the only time Blochmann dared to be frank with him was shortly before her death in 1969: "I am a little helpless confronted with the 'Question of Thinking.' All this is alien to my common sense. For once I must tell you this, dear Martin, even if it disappoints you. . . . My way of looking at the matters of life is . . . so distant from your philosophical viewpoint that, I am afraid, we have a common language only in a limited if also valuable realm."[118]

By 1955 Heidegger had regained his former authority even though his political past occasionally fell under attack. Five years before, he had needed Arendt to listen to him, to absolve him and help restore his reputation. Now it seems that he did not want to be reminded by her presence of that 1950 meeting and his position as a penitent. It belonged to the past, and he saw no reason to revive it. Arendt's friendship with Jaspers continued to annoy him. And it certainly was not worthwhile for him anymore to upset his wife. Heidegger's behavior distressed Arendt, but she was gaining distance as well. Unemotionally, she reported to Bluecher: "Intellectually not much is going on [in Germany] except for a spectacular renaissance of everything classic. Otherwise still only Heidegger, but even this is quite disgusting inasmuch as people either present it [Heidegger's philosophy] as sheer nonsense or imitate him in the most improbable fashion. To what extent he encourages it himself, I don't know. Loewith told me, with no venom (Heidegger's picture hangs in his study), that Heidegger organizes seminars for professors in a farm building in Todtnauberg, and there, so to speak, 'hammers' his philosophy."[119]

Arendt's decision not to see Heidegger on her trip to Germany in 1955 was a watershed in their relationship. Initially she had just wanted to "let the grass grow a little," but the grass would give way to brush and the brush to forest before she saw him again. She would be sixty-one years old, he seventy-eight.

During all these years he was a constant presence in her thoughts and in her work. She could not regard him only as her teacher and a philosopher. Their shared past did not vanish. She had to reconcile herself to Elfride Heidegger's predominant position in his life, which dwarfed her own and which, Heidegger made it clear, was what he wanted. The turbulence that her visits were certain to cause appeared to outweigh all other considerations for him. He no longer was willing to meet with Arendt—because of his wife, because of Arendt's fame or her friendship with Jaspers, or because of the recent or long-ago past. She no longer made an effort to see him on her frequent trips to Germany.

Within Arendt nothing had changed, however. Heidegger could make her suffer, he could give her joy. Steadfastly she clung to her friendship with him and tolerated no interference. While visiting Karl Jaspers in October 1956, "I finally had a sort of general discussion with Jaspers," she informed Bluecher, "in the course of which he presented me with an ultimatum involving Heidegger." Jaspers demanded that she sever her ties with Heidegger. "I became furious and told him I will not accept any ultimatums."[120]

Jaspers had already lost hope of a reconciliation with Heidegger, and it disturbed him that Arendt showed no regard for his all but broken relationship with Heidegger. Jaspers maintained that he had not decided after 1945 never to see Heidegger again; "it just so happened."[121] But it was more complicated than that. He initiated the correspondence between them in 1949 (two letters written in 1942 and 1948 remained unsent), and at the beginning of 1950 he wrote, "I hope as you do that when the opportunity arises we will meet again and talk."[122] Heidegger was delighted by the "dreaming boy" vision Jaspers had had of him in the Nazi time. He described in his last long letter to Jaspers—written 8 April 1950, two months after Arendt's first visit—the betrayal of his dreams, the ordeal he had gone through, the courage he had shown defying the regime in his lectures.* "[N]o one took such risks as I did."[123] He stressed the crucial role his wife played in his distancing himself from the Nazi regime, perhaps to fend off Arendt's report about his wife's abusive, antisemitic remarks which, he suspected, she may have repeated to Jaspers. So eager was he at least to "shake hands" with Jaspers that he offered to meet the train Jaspers would take if he came to Heidelberg.[124]

It took Jaspers two years to answer this letter, which was

*In his letter of 4 November 1945 to the rector of the University of Freiburg, he wrote: "There was nothing special about my spiritual resistance during the last eleven years." Heidegger, "An das Akademische Rektorat . . . " See also R. Wolin., ed., *Heidegger Controversy,* 66.

filled with self-serving justifications, half-truths, and facts that did "not always correspond with my recollections," Jaspers wrote in his reply. But it was Heidegger's statement on Stalin—"Stalin does not have to declare a war anymore. He wins a battle every day. But nobody sees it. There is no escape for us"—that provoked Jaspers's ire. "To read something like this frightens me," he wrote. Didn't Heidegger understand that Germany had paved the way for Stalin's victory? he asked. Didn't he see that a philosophy which leads to a "monstrous vision" of even more destruction prepares the ground for yet another victory for totalitarianism, just as "philosophy . . . before 1933 actually prepared the ground to accept Hitler?" "Hannah's splendid book" [*The Origins of Totalitarianism*] discussed these associations, he said, to make plain the gulf between Heidegger's viewpoint and that of his student and the affinity between himself and Arendt.[125]

But when in 1953 Heidegger congratulated Jaspers on his seventieth birthday and asked him to "accept this greeting from a wanderer," Jaspers again softened.[126] He commiserated with Heidegger, who, he saw from his letter, felt "all alone." With undisguised nostalgia he wrote, "I see you before me as though it were just now, when you were often together with me, with us, ever since 1920. . . . I see your gestures, your glance, I hear your voice." The tone of Heidegger's letter stirred anew a hope of "what could still be possible between us."[127]

A reconciliation was not to be. Though "*der Knabe*" (the

boy) still held an allure for Jaspers, though he himself petitioned to lift the ban on Heidegger's teaching, though he kept writing letters he never sent, he knew, as is evident from his notes, that Heidegger never parted with the Nazi ideology, that he was not to be trusted. The notes he wrote to himself about Heidegger for almost the rest of his life (published as *Notizen zu Martin Heidegger,* Hans Saner, ed., 1978) show a man torn between his desire to be close to Heidegger again and his overwhelming need to remain faithful to his principles. According to Saner, Jaspers waited twenty years for Heidegger's public renunciation of fascism, and only after Hannah Arendt told him that Heidegger would deny any guilt until his dying day did Jaspers finally give up on reconciliation.[128] For Heidegger it was rather a matter of pragmatism and self-interest to show the world that a man of Jaspers's integrity believed in his short-lived "error" and had absolved him of any wrong-doing; to claim Jaspers as a friend would have been his ultimate victory, and it would have eliminated or at least seriously weakened the attacks against him.

The rift with Heidegger was to remain permanent. "I remember many conversations with Jaspers [about Heidegger] until the last months of his life," Saner recalls.[129] When in 1961 Arendt was reading the galley proofs of Heidegger's "important and beautiful" book on Nietzsche for his American publisher and her friend, Kurt Wolff, she did not mention it to Jaspers lest she upset the ailing elderly man.[130]

In 1958, Karl Jaspers turned seventy-five. His newly published book *The Atom Bomb and the Future of Mankind* won him the Peace Prize of the German Book Trade Association, to be bestowed at a grand ceremony in Frankfurt's famous Paul's Church. Arendt, much to her surprise and joy but also discomfiture, was invited to deliver the address accompanying the prize. She had doubts about the propriety of having a personal friend, a woman, a Jew, and a non-German deliver the eulogy, and, as she admitted to Bluecher, she was scared. But her foremost concern was Heidegger. "I cannot tell Jaspers about it," she wrote Bluecher. She was apprehensive about being "forced" to make an unequivocal public statement likely to be interpreted as an act of solidarity with Jaspers and a repudiation of Heidegger. But, she comforted herself, "I can talk and say as I please."[131]

When Heidegger turned seventy a year later, Arendt sent him wishes from herself and Bluecher, posted in Basel. In a brief acknowledgment mailed to New York, Heidegger included his wife's greetings and pointed out that the note was deliberately not sent to Basel. He knew of course that Arendt was visiting Jaspers, and he missed no opportunity to let her know that he did not appreciate her divided loyalty. She placed herself between two men who loathed and admired each other, both of whom had a claim on her, both of whom resented that she alone maintained the continuity of friendship with Heidegger *and* with Jaspers.

The Human Condition, published in the United States in 1958, grew out of Arendt's thinking on man's political activities—action and speech as distinguished from work

and labor. The German translation, published as *Vita activa,*
came out in 1960. In a brief letter of 28 October 1960,
Arendt informed Heidegger that she had requested her publisher to send him a copy. "You will notice," she wrote him,
"that there is no dedication in the book. Had the relations
between us not been star-crossed—but I mean *between,* that
is neither you nor me—I would have asked you whether I
may have dedicated it to you; the book evolved directly from
the first Marburg days* and it owes you just about everything
in every regard. As things are this seemed to me impossible;
but I did want at least to tell you, in one way or another, the
bare facts."

On a separate sheet of paper Arendt wrote a verse that she
never sent:

Re Vita Activa
The dedication of this book is left out.
How could I dedicate it to you,
my trusted friend,
to whom I remained faithful
and unfaithful,
And both in love.[132]

This was, in all probability, Arendt's first letter to Heidegger (except for seasonal or birthday wishes) after a six-year
silence. Sad but honest, it provoked Heidegger's wrath.

*In the original Arendt wrote "Freiburg," a telling mistake that is
corrected here by the author.

In the summer of 1961, after attending Adolf Eichmann's trial in Jerusalem, which she was covering for *The New Yorker,* Arendt flew to Switzerland to see Jaspers and his wife, and from there she proceeded to Germany. In Heidelberg she discussed the trial with students and faculty members and then went to Freiburg. Perhaps she was hoping that Heidegger, after receiving her confessional note reminding him of their Marburg days, paying homage to his mentorship, and admitting to the pain still wracking her, would be pleased to see her, maybe even eager to welcome his old faithful friend.

"I had written to Heidegger . . . where he could reach me," she wrote to Jaspers. "He did not get in touch with me, which did not particularly surprise me, since I didn't even know whether he was in town." But then a law professor from the University of Freiburg, Joseph H. Kaiser, invited her to his "extravagantly luxurious" residence, which, Arendt discovered, he shared with a male lover. At Arendt's request he also invited Eugen Fink, a professor of philosophy and colleague of Husserl and Heidegger, whom she had known since her university days. Fink "turned down the invitation—'brusquely'; he had no desire to see me, in fact distinctly hinting that it was Heidegger who had apparently forbidden him to accept it. Why? No idea. . . . A year ago Heidegger sent me his recent publications with an inscription. In response I sent him *Vita activa.* C'est tout. [That's all.]"[133]

Were this indeed all, Heidegger might not have avoided her or instructed Fink to decline the invitation. Evidently he interpreted the withholding of the dedication and the explanation accompanying it as an act of arrogance, an accusation, and, worse, a decision Arendt made alone even though it involved them both. This had never happened before. Enraged, he punished her bluntly and publicly for daring to think and to act as an independent person.

Three months later, after Bluecher had recuperated from a grave illness caused by congenital aneurysm, Arendt wrote Jaspers: "Heidegger: yes, it is a most annoying story. It has nothing to do with the eulogy [as Jaspers had meantime suggested], since I was in touch with him afterwards. Nor do I think his wife was involved. . . . I know that he finds unbearable that my name appears in public, that I write books, etc. Always, I have been virtually lying to him about myself, pretending the books, the name, did not exist, and I couldn't, so to speak, count to three, unless it concerned the interpretations of his works. Then, he would be quite pleased if it turned out that I can count to three and sometimes to four. But suddenly I became bored with the cheating and got a punch in the nose. For a while I was absolutely furious, but no more. Instead, I think I had somehow deserved what I got—both for the cheating and for abruptly ending the game."[134] The letter she wrote to Heidegger in October, the real cause of the whole affair, as she well knew, remained unmentioned. But she explained the heart of the matter: that she chose to tell Heidegger the unvarnished truth about their relationship, that she no longer was prepared to play the game by his rules.

Jaspers was astonished, and not without reason. Unaware of Arendt's letter to Heidegger concerning the dedication, he was searching in the dark. Heidegger "must have known about your books for a long time. . . . [T]he only new element is that this one [*Vita activa*] he received directly from you—and what a reaction!"[135]

Heidegger not only knew about her books, but he also had them at home; he unfailingly informed Arendt that his wife enjoyed them, though his inadequate knowledge of English prevented him from reading them himself. There is no indication in his letters that he read the German translations. He also knew about her work from her letters. So he knew that she could count to three and even to four. It was her act of independence that was a visible sign that she was slipping from his control. Her successful and fulfilled life deprived Heidegger of a worshipful disciple. Perhaps he could regain control if he brought her to her senses. He never learned of the Arendt who remained "faithful and unfaithful, and both in love."

Five years after this incident, in 1966, Jaspers revealed to Arendt facts about Heidegger that he had withheld from her for twenty years. In February 1966, *Der Spiegel* published an article critical of Heidegger's Nazi past and his antisemitism. Casually, Arendt asked Jaspers what he thought about it. "I didn't like it at all," she wrote him. "He should be left in peace."[136] The eighty-three-year-old Jaspers fired back:

I do not think it is desirable to 'leave Heidegger in peace.' He is a powerful presence, and one that everyone who wants an excuse for his own Nazi past wants to fall back on. . . . The claim that Heidegger stopped coming to us because Gertrud is Jewish is pure invention. . . . Gertrud's Jewishness certainly was not the reason. But at his last visit in May 1933 he treated her in an exceptionally discourteous fashion. He left hardly saying good-bye to her. The reason was that she, as is her way, had spoken her mind openly and clearly, whereas I had spoken cautiously, indirectly, and with great mistrust. I have never forgotten his ungallant behavior to Gertrud in that situation. . . . I consider the reason that he gave after 1945, namely that he was ashamed [to come], an excuse. . . . Before my 60th birthday [Friedrich] Oehlkers, our friend, professor of botany at Freiburg, told him that my birthday was forthcoming and asked if he wished to convey his good wishes. Heidegger spoke very emotionally about me and said yes, of course. He did not do it. Just as he said nothing when I was stripped of my office in 1937. . . . Of course I take a different view of what he did objectively. How did he, never an antisemite himself, behave toward the Jews: sometimes superbly, when he wanted to protect someone like Brock [Werner Brock, Heidegger's assistant] (as by the way, almost all the old Nazis did); and sometimes, as in his official letter to Goettingen about the Jew Fraenkel, he would use exactly the same language as the Nazis did. . . . His behavior toward Husserl was another case of obedience to the Nazis. . . . I have just read Heidegger's answer in *Der Spiegel*. I found it irritating and medi-ocre.[137]

Demonstrating once again the ineradicable bond she felt with Heidegger, Arendt refused to accept Jaspers's accusa-tions. Rather, they fueled her indignation against Heideg-ger's critics and again moved her to defend him. "You said yourself that [Heidegger's] antisemitism was not an issue. But the attacks on him come straight from that quarter and not another." She suspected, she wrote, "though I cannot prove it," that the "stringpullers" were members of the Adorno-Horkheimer circle in Frankfurt. Theodor W. Adorno, a "half-Jew and one of the most repugnant people I know,"* or Max Horkheimer, or people instigated by them, were perfectly capable, she asserted, of destroying Heidegger. "For years every single person in Germany who is in opposi-tion to them is accused of antisemitism or threatened to be accused."[138]

As for Jaspers's painfully long-kept secrets about Heideg-ger's rude treatment of Gertrud Jaspers, the "Jew Fraenkel" jargon, and Heidegger's servile behavior toward the Nazis, Arendt wrote them off in one brief sentence: "No one has the slightest idea about the things you have said."[139] It followed that if Jaspers continued to abstain from publicly telling the

*Arendt always referred to Adorno as Wiesengrund, his real name, to emphasize his attempt to conceal his Jewish origin. Adorno was his mother's maiden name.

truth, Heidegger's reputation would not be further jeopardized, and it would seem that Jaspers did not support the accusation. Some of the evidence remained undisclosed because Heidegger's two best friends cooperated in keeping it secret. But, as Faulkner said, the past is never dead. It is not even past.

In 1966 Hannah Arendt turned sixty years old. After years of silence Heidegger wrote her a long letter—though he passed over in silence the prestigious Lessing Prize she was awarded in 1959—a signal that he had let bygones be bygones. He informed her that he and Elfride had made three pleasant trips to Greece, rather late in life in view of the role of the Greek philosophers and ancient Greece in his work. But Heidegger did not like to travel to foreign countries; he felt most comfortable in the Todtnauberg "*Huette*" (cabin), where for years there was no electricity, and the water was fetched from a well. Along with the letter, he sent Arendt a picture of the landscape he saw from his study in the cabin, birthday greetings, and a poem by Hoelderlin called "Autumn."

Indeed, it was autumn. Heidegger was seventy-seven, his wife seventy-three. Karl Jaspers, plagued by various ailments and deafness, would die in three years at the age of eighty-six, without a reconciliation with Heidegger. The time of *Sturm und Drang* was over.

Heidegger's letter brought Arendt "the greatest joy," she responded within days.[140] On the back page of a draft of her grateful letter, accompanied by a quotation from Goethe—their inner world had undergone no change—she listed publications to be included in Heidegger's collected works. She had been planning that venture for years, trying to obtain an agreement from the reluctant author. He was uninterested in following the trodden path, he wrote her, and having "Heideggeriana," as he ruefully referred to his works, collected. The selection presented another problem: he refused to cut himself off from his past openly, but neither did he want to have the compromising articles, speeches, and statements published.

A year later, in 1967, Arendt paid the Heideggers a visit, her first since 1952. It was followed by several warm and lively letters from Heidegger and by his book, published in 1960, *Der Ursprung des Kunstwerks* (The Origin of the Work of Art), with an inscription: "For Hannah, in memory of meeting again, Martin, Frg. 27 July 1967."[141] After they met in 1950, Heidegger sent Arendt five of his works, all warmly inscribed, and though he sent her many more books over the years (sometimes they were sent directly by the publisher without an inscription), this one came after a years-long interruption. It had a special meaning for her: she did her utmost to start the healing process, late though it was in their lives, but she succeeded. She probably couldn't bear the thought that Heidegger might die with things between them "star-crossed." Without making peace with Elfride Heidegger, Arendt knew, the healing had no chance. So she extended her hand to Heidegger's wife, they agreed to call each other by their first names, a sign of true closeness, and the barrier that first appeared in Arendt's life when she was eighteen was, in a sense, removed. It was a generous act of friendship toward Heidegger, characteristic of her profound, unshakable concept of what the word *friend* meant. It was also an admission that her feelings for Heidegger remained intact. Heidegger, she knew, was more and more often in low spirits, and that was when he needed her. The two poems he composed for her toward the end of the year bore the portentous titles "In the Darkness" and "Evening Song."

The following year Arendt was busy supervising the English translation of his *What Is Called Thinking?* "So help him to ask it," Bluecher had urged her in 1952, "one of the most wonderful philosophical questions after God." Heidegger wrote to her, gracefully acknowledging that her help was an act of friendship, adding that no one understood his thought better than she did. Of course she had heard this before in different forms, but every time he said it he confirmed, she thought, their inner bond. Heidegger read her article on Walter Benjamin—though fleetingly, he admitted—and it received praise from him, the first and the last, it seems.

The next year Arendt came again to see the Heideggers, and in 1969 Heinrich Bluecher and his wife paid a visit to Martin Heidegger and his wife. The unusual occasion was commemorated by a special gift from Heidegger: a booklet published in Messkirch, written by Fritz Heidegger, to celebrate the eightieth birthday of the town's most famous son. Heidegger's inscription said: "For Hannah and Heinrich— Martin and Elfride."[142] The circle was closed.

The two couples planned a similar visit for the following year. In October 1970, Heinrich Bluecher died.

In April 1969, Elfride Heidegger turned to Arendt for help. Her husband's declining health made it imperative that they sell their big house and build a smaller, one-story building, she wrote. The estimated cost was DM 80,000 to 100,000. They did not have that amount of money, so they decided to sell the manuscript of *Being and Time*. Neither of them understood anything about money, she wrote, nor did they know how much the manuscript was worth or where to sell it.* If need be, the manuscript of the Nietzsche lectures could be sold as well, Heidegger asked his wife to add at the end of her letter. The matter must be handled with utmost discretion, Elfride Heidegger stressed.

In five days Arendt answered: she did not know anything about buying and selling manuscripts, but as far as she could judge, the *Being and Time* manuscript was no doubt of great value and would appreciate with time. Such manuscripts should therefore be offered to collectors rather than to official institutions. To obtain reliable information the Heideggers should turn to the respectable auction house J. A. Stargardt in Marburg. Discretion was out of the question since the house sends catalogues all over the world. But one could find a middleman. Arendt offered to talk to some people she trusted, including the director of the manuscript division at the Library of Congress. Her advice pointed them above all to keeping the manuscript in Germany.

*The correspondence between Jaspers and Heidegger provides some evidence to the contrary: the conversion of foreign currency into deutsche marks, for instance, an issue for Heidegger when he received a job offer from Japan in 1924, presented no difficulties for him. See Biemel and Saner, *Heidegger / Jaspers Briefwechsel*, 48.

In three days Elfride Heidegger's response arrived. Auctioning did not seem the right way to proceed, she wrote; rather, a foundation or a library like the Library of Congress seemed an appropriate buyer. Could Arendt do them a favor, if it was not too much trouble, and find out from the experienced librarian she had mentioned, how much money the manuscript could fetch? No further correspondence on the subject was necessary in view of the Bluechers' forthcoming August visit, when things could be discussed in private.

Nonetheless, Arendt wrote on 17 May an exhaustive two-page, single-spaced letter, a summary of the advice she had received from the librarian. She said that she wanted to relay the information at once, while it was fresh in her memory. The natural place to house the invaluable manuscript was, according to him, the Schiller Literaturarchiv in Marbach am Neckar, which had large funds at its disposal; next he suggested the Bibliothèque Nationale in Paris, known for its vast holdings of German manuscripts; and, in the United States, Yale University (famous for its German collections, including that of Rilke), or Princeton or Harvard Universities. The highest price could probably be fetched at the University of Texas, which was eager to build its assets; the Library of Congress buys only Americana. Arendt repeated her first suggestion that they turn to the Stargardt auction house, which also acted as an agent. Another possibility, she said, was the experienced and trustworthy professor Koester from the German Library in Frankfurt, the successor of Professor Eppelsheimer, who was enormously helpful when in 1949 Arendt came to Germany to identify the "abandoned" (*herrenlos*) Jewish cultural property. There is no sure answer, she wrote, as to how much the manuscript could fetch; some Einstein letters of no great interest sold at Sotheby's in London for £5,000; Gerhard Hauptmann's papers were sold in Berlin for more than DM 2.5 million. The librarian estimated that *Being and Time* could fetch between DM 70,000 and 100,000 at the least.[143]

There seems to be more to the exchange about selling Heidegger's manuscript than meets the eye. To whom do the Heideggers turn when money is concerned? To a Jew, one in whose blood it is to be well versed in pecuniary matters. One might attribute to Heidegger's ill health his inability to calculate his finances were it not for the fact that later, in even worse health, he exacted a stiff price for all his manuscripts when he sold them to the Schiller Literaturarchiv in Marbach am Neckar.

Arendt recognized the pattern when she saw it. Why not sell the manuscript in Germany, where it rightfully belonged? Would a good German deprive his country of a priceless script for the sake of a few more dollars? Arendt's suggestion that the Heideggers sell it to the Schiller Literaturarchiv or the National Archiv in Frankfurt was turned down by Elfride Heidegger with the explanation that the Germans would not pay as much as the Americans.

Arendt would do anything to help Martin Heidegger, who now, toward the end of his life, again needed her for reasons less lofty than spiritual affinity. But she was irked by the role that he and his wife—she probably suspected that Elfride Heidegger was the driving force behind the idea—imposed on her. She knew as little about buying and selling as they did, she told them. That is why she made a point of seeking professional advice and merely relaying the results. Heidegger, with his lifelong contempt for America and its idol—money—made a strange partner in this venture. He shrank neither from acquiring American dollars nor from depriving his country of a national treasure.

Arendt's mixed feelings about getting involved in buying and selling might also be seen in her reference to her first trip to Germany to recover the Hebraica and Judaica stolen by the Germans. She used the word *herrenlos,* "abandoned" or "ownerless," the euphemism invented by the Nazis in order to cover up looting, to describe the Jewish property.[144] Was her use of the term a reminder for Elfride Heidegger that Hannah Arendt had not forgotten the past? Perhaps.

Fourteen

Nine days after Heinrich Bluecher died in October 1970, Martin and Elfride Heidegger offered Arendt their condolences. Attached to the letter was a poem called "Time," composed by Heidegger. The following summer she paid them a visit. She would come regularly every year for the rest of her life. The visits were planned by Elfride Heidegger, down to the month, day, and hour. Heidegger's health was further declining, but his depressions could sometimes be assuaged by Arendt's presence. In 1973, Walter Biemel, one of Heidegger's disciples, asked Arendt to write to him. Heidegger was worried that she might have borne him a grudge because she had failed to drop him a note before leaving Germany. At the time she had planned to visit he was staying with his brother in Messkirch, and he felt very badly about missing her. He saw practically no one, since contact with the outside was regulated by Frau Heidegger, who in principle allowed no visitors. While this restriction was perhaps necessary on account of his ill health, as Biemel ventured to guess, the loneliness was taking a heavy toll on him.

Elfride Heidegger, who turned eighty in 1973, certainly had a hard time trying to accommodate her husband. Heidegger complained to Arendt that having too many visitors exhausted him. He needed to decide whom he wished or did not wish to see and to find a balance between a flood of visitors and no visitors at all. But it probably was impossible to establish any guidelines, for Heidegger's condition and mood kept fluctuating. He was eager to see Arendt, however. Now he even wanted her to come twice a year, at the beginning and end of her European tour.

Heidegger conducted his last seminar in the fall of 1973. The preparation, which occupied all of August and the beginning of September, and the delivery—two to two and a half hours over three days—were so strenuous that he had to call off Arendt's visit. She would understand, he wrote her, that he did it only reluctantly; he expected her to come early the next year, when he would have a chance to share with her some new thoughts on Parmenides that occurred to him only at the last seminar session. Thinking, he wrote, still gave him much pleasure.

In his last years Heidegger's letters to Hannah Arendt became warm and caring. Written in a simple yet elegant prose, they reflected the mood of a serene but not mellow man who had put his battles, if not his weapons, behind him. Seldom would the old mixture of perfidy and sentimentality seep through, as when he mentioned a birthday gift (the collected works of Goethe) that his wife had given him in 1917, long before he met Hannah Arendt. He still had the power to hurt her. His letters concerning royalties— Heidegger had a firm grasp of his finances—contractual stipulations, or publishers' obligations were meticulous and businesslike and put ever new demands on Arendt. Yet for the first time Heidegger became genuinely interested in Arendt's life, in her work, even in her success. Though he had ignored her winning of the Lessing Prize, he now expressed regret at missing the press descriptions of the ceremony in Copenhagen where Arendt was honored in 1975 with the coveted Danish Sonning Prize for Contributions to European Civilization. And he invited her to celebrate, though belatedly, the occasion at her forthcoming visit with a glass of good wine. He knew in detail what she was teaching (he had read the syllabi she sent him), what she was reading, how her work was progressing, what was her timetable. Especially in the last two years they were sharing, as never before, thoughts on Life and on their own lives. He would advise her (as Bluecher had) to make a stop to rest in Basel before continuing her trip, lest she overexert herself. It pleased him that she read Goethe. It angered him that so few other people did. Could Goethe's thought still be saved? But for whom?

Throughout 1971, Arendt wrote Heidegger extensive letters; working on the posthumously published *Life of the Mind,* she asked him questions about thinking, willing, and judging. The following year she returned to the question of evil. The English translation of his works, his royalties, his publishers, and the collection of his works were always on her mind. Only in 1974 would Heidegger agree to have his collected works published, in strict accordance with his instructions. From Mary McCarthy's house in Castine, Maine, where she was spending the first summer after her husband's death, she insisted that he publish a collection of his essays tentatively called *Reflections,* a title Heidegger did not like. She tried to convince him that "regardless of anything personal, your years-long friendship with Jaspers—regardless of the course the friendship took later—belongs to the history of philosophy in Germany in our century."[145]

The smaller house built with the money obtained from selling the manuscript (to the Schiller Literaturarchiv) was finished, and much to Arendt's relief the Heideggers moved in. To celebrate the occasion she sent a gift of flowers. Arendt and Heidegger tried to give each other some joy: Arendt sent him Nadezhda Mandelstam's *Hope Against Hope* and Melville's *Billy Budd*. Heidegger gave her tips on books to read, offered poems and flowers, generously advised her on her work. Now their letters provided them both with comfort. Heidegger worried about Arendt's exhaustion and sadness, conditions, he stressed, that he knew all too well. But there was not much he could do to console her. There is a tone of resignation in this exchange.

"No one can deliver a lecture the way you do, nor did anyone before you," Arendt wrote him in 1974, revisiting the lectures she attended half a century before and musing about the time she had sat in his classroom.[146] The next year she spent several months in the Marbach archive working on Jaspers's literary estate, and Heidegger was deeply disappointed that she left Germany without seeing him once more.

In her last letter to Heidegger, written on 27 July 1975 from Tegna in Switzerland, where she was spending a working vacation, Hannah Arendt promised to come to Freiburg in August. In his last letter to her, written on 30 July,

Heidegger expressed his joy at seeing her soon. She was expected on the 12th or 15th of August, between 3 and 4 P.M., and, as usual, she was to stay for supper. She came to see him in mid-August.

On 4 December 1975, Hannah Arendt died. Martin Heidegger survived her by five months. He died on 28 May 1976.

Notes

Abbreviations

The following abbreviations are used in the notes:

A   Hannah Arendt
B   Heinrich Bluecher
H   Martin Heidegger
LC   Library of Congress
ALT   Hannah Arendt Literary Trust

The correspondence between Hannah Arendt and Heinrich Bluecher is used by permission of the Hannah Arendt Literary Trust. It is deposited in the Library of Congress, Washington, D.C. Letters from Hannah Arendt to Martin Heidegger and to Elfride Heidegger are used by permission of the Hannah Arendt Literary Trust. Martin Heidegger's letters to Hannah Arendt were perused with the permission of the Hannah Arendt Literary Trust.

Introduction

1. A to H, 28 October 1960, not sent, ALT.

2. A to B, August 1945, LC.

3. Lotte Kohler and Hans Saner, eds., *Hannah Arendt / Karl Jaspers Briefwechsel 1926–1969* (Munich: Piper, 1985), 233–237.

4. A to H, 8 May 1954, ALT.

5. A to H, 26 July 1974, ALT.

6. A to B, 8 February 1950, LC.

Hannah Arendt / Martin Heidegger

1. Interview with Hugo Ott, Freiburg, Germany, 1 August 1991.

2. *New York Review of Books,* 21 October 1971. First published in German magazine *Merkur* in 1969, when Heidegger turned eighty.

3. Karl Loewith, *Mein Leben in Deutschland vor und nach 1939* (Stuttgart: Metzler, 1986), 42–43.

4. Fritz Heidegger, "Martin Heidegger zum 80 Geburtstag von seiner Heimatstadt Messkirch" (Frankfurt am Main: Klostermann, 1969), 60.

5. Walter Beimel and Hans Saner, eds., *Martin Heidegger / Karl Jaspers Briefwechsel 1920–1963* (Frankfurt am Main: Klostermann; Munich: Piper, 1990), 46.

6. Interview with Kaete Fuerst, Ramat Hasharon, Israel, 13 January 1990.

7. A to H, 9 February 1950, ALT.

8. A to H, 28 October 1960, ALT.

9. Hugo Ott, *Martin Heidegger, Unterwegs zu seiner Biographie* (Frankfurt / New York: Campus Verlag, 1988), 183.

10. Letter to the author from Melvyn Hill, 3 March 1993.

11. A to B, 18 September 1937, LC.

12. Interview with Kaete Fuerst, Ramat Hasharon, Israel, 13 January 1990.

13. A to B, 8 February 1950, LC.

14. Hannah Arendt, *Denktagebuch,* 1953, ALT.

15. Joachim W. Storck, ed., *Martin Heidegger / Elisabeth Blochmann Briefwechsel 1918−1969* (Marbach am Neckar: Deutsche Schillergesellschaft, 1989), 22−23.

16. A to H, 22 April 1928, ALT.

17. Elke Schubert, ed., *Guenther Anders antwortet* (Berlin: Tiamat, 1927), 24.

18. Ibid., 24−25.

19. A to H, undated, probably spring 1929, ALT.

20. A to H, undated, probably September 1929, ALT.

21. Ulrich Sieg, "Die Verjudung des deutschen Geistes, Ein unbekannter Brief Heideggers" (2 October 1929), *Die Zeit,* 29 December 1989.

22. A to B, 11 August 1936, LC.

23. B to A, 12 August 1936, LC.

24. A to B, 19 August 1936, LC.

25. B to A, 12 August 1936, LC; A to B, 19 August 1936, LC.

26. B to A, August 1936.

27. A to B, 12 August 1936, LC.

28. A to B, 24 August 1936, LC.

29. A to B, 24 November 1936 and 26 November 1936, LC.

30. A to B, 18 September 1937, LC.

31. Ibid.

32. B to A, 21 August 1936, LC.

33. A to B, 19 August 1936, LC.

34. B to A, 19 September 1937, LC.

35. A to B, 20 February 1937, LC.

36. Biemel and Saner, *Heidegger / Jaspers Briefwechsel,* 213.

37. A to B, 26 December 1949, LC.

38. Kohler and Saner, *Arendt / Jaspers Briefwechsel,* 204.

39. Hans Saner, ed., *Karl Jaspers Notizen zu Martin Heidegger* (Munich: Piper, 1978), 7.

40. Ibid., 141.

41. Karl Jaspers, *Philosophische Autobiographie* (Munich: Piper, 1977), 97.

42. Biemel and Saner, *Heidegger / Jaspers Briefwechsel,* 42.

43. Saner, *Jaspers Notizen,* 92.

44. Ibid., 87.

45. Jaspers, *Philosophische Autobiographie,* 101.

46. Biemel and Saner, *Heidegger / Jaspers Briefwechsel,* 156.

47. Ibid., 146–147.

48. Ibid., 196.

49. Ibid., 197.

50. Ibid., 196–198.

51. A to B, 24 May 1952, LC.

52. Adolf Hitler, *Mein Kampf* (Munich: Zentralverlag d.NSDAP, 1940), 414.

53. Ott, *Heidegger,* 183.

54. Ibid., 316.

55. Guenther Neske, Emil Kettering, eds., *Antwort, Martin Heidegger im Gespraech* (Pfullingen: Guenther Neske, 1988), 206.

56. Ibid., 206–207.

57. Ott, *Heidegger,* 201–213.

58. Martin Heidegger, "An das Akademische Rektorat der Albert-Ludwig Universitaet," 4 November 1945, ALT; also in Richard Wolin, ed., *The Heidegger Controversy* (New York: Columbia University Press, 1991), 61–66.

59. Ott, *Heidegger,* 211.

60. A to B, 13 June 1952, LC.

61. Storck, *Heidegger / Blochmann Briefwechsel,* 90.

62. Friedrich Oehlkers to Karl Jaspers, 15 December 1945, courtesy of Hugo Ott; also in Ott, *Heidegger,* 135.

63. Storck, *Heidegger / Blochmann Briefwechsel,* 71.

64. Loewith, *Mein Leben,* 57.

65. Ott, *Heidegger,* 295.

66. Ibid., 280–287.

67. Martin Heidegger, "An das Akademische Rektorat . . . " ALT.

68. Ott, *Heidegger,* 250.

69. Martin Heidegger, "An das Akademische Rektorat . . . " ALT.

70. Jaspers, *Philosophische Autobiographie,* 102.

71. Ott, *Heidegger,* 322–323.

72. Hannah Arendt, "What Is Existenz Philosophy?" *Partisan Review,* no. 1 (1946): 46.

73. Kohler and Saner, *Arendt / Jaspers Briefwechsel,* 79.

74. Ibid., 84.

75. Ibid., 178.

76. Ibid., 204.

77. A to B, 18 December 1949, LC.

78. A to B, 3 January 1950, LC.

79. A to B, 5 February 1950, LC.

80. A to H, 9 February 1950, ALT.

81. A to B, 8 February 1950, LC.

82. Kohler and Saner, *Arendt / Jaspers Briefwechsel,* 204.

83. A to H, 9 February 1950, ALT.

84. A to B, 8 February 1950, LC.

85. A to H, 9 February 1950, ALT.

86. A to Elfride Heidegger, 10 February 1950, ALT.

87. A to B, 7 March 1950, LC.

88. B to A, 10 May 1952, LC; A to B, 18 May 1952, LC.

89. A to B, 24 April 1952, LC.

90. A to B, 24 May 1952, LC.

91. B to A, 29 May 1952, LC.

92. B to A, 5 July 1952, LC.

93. A to B, 30 May 1952, LC.

94. A to B, 6 June 1952, LC.

95. A to B, 13 June 1952, LC.

96. B to A, 14 June 1952, LC.

97. A to B, 20 June 1952, LC.

98. A to B, 13 June 1952, LC.

99. B to A, 21 June 1952, LC.

100. A to B, 26 June 1952, LC.

101. A to B, 1 July 1952, LC.

102. A to B, 26 June 1952, LC.

103. B to A, 28 June 1952, LC.

104. A to B, 25 July 1952, LC.

105. A to B, 18 July 1952, LC.

106. A to the Rev. John M. Oesterreicher, 23 August 1952, ALT.

107. Kohler and Saner, *Arendt / Jaspers Briefwechsel,* 368.

108. A to H, 8 May 1954, ALT.

109. A to B, 25 May 1955, LC.

110. A to B, 14 November 1955, LC.

111. B to A, end of November 1955, LC.

112. A to B, 28 November 1955, LC.

113. B to A, beginning of December 1955, LC.

114. Ott, *Heidegger,* 305.

115. Storck, *Heidegger / Blochmann Briefwechsel,* 72.

116. Ibid., 104.

117. Ibid., 102–103.

118. Ibid., 120.

119. A to B, 28 November 1955, LC.

120. A to B, 31 October 1956, LC.

121. Kohler and Saner, *Arendt / Jaspers Briefwechsel,* 666.

122. Biemel and Saner, *Heidegger / Jaspers Briefwechsel,* 198.

123. Ibid., 202.

124. Ibid., 203.

125. Ibid., 207–211.

126. Ibid., 212.

127. Ibid., 213.

128. Jaspers, *Notizen,* 7.

129. Ibid., 7.

130. A to B, 28 May 1961, LC.

131. A to B, 25 May 1958, LC.

132. A to H, 28 October 1960.

133. Kohler and Saner, *Arendt / Jaspers Briefwechsel,* 484.

134. Ibid., 494.

135. Ibid., 496.

136. Ibid., 663.

137. Ibid., 665–666.

138. Ibid., 669–670.

139. Ibid.

140. A to H, 16 October 1966, ALT.

141. Heidegger's inscription, Martin Heidegger Archiv, Deutsches Literaturachiv, Marbach am Neckar.

142. Ibid.

143. A to Elfride Heidegger, 17 May 1969, ALT.

144. Ibid.

145. A to H, 28 July 1971, ALT.

146. A to H, 26 July 1974, ALT.

A Note on the Type

This book was set in Monotype Perpetua, a digitized
version of the typeface originally designed by Eric Gill
between 1925 and 1930. The italic, designed later, was
originally named Felicity.

Composed by The Composing Room of Michigan, Inc.
of Grand Rapids. Printed in the United States of America by BookCrafters, Inc., of Chelsea, Michigan.
Designed by Nancy Ovedovitz.

B   3/98
Are   10.00

Ettinger, Hannah

Hannah Arendt, Martin Heidegger

DATE DUE